re

& others

washington d.c.
& environs

REVISED EDITION

published in cooperation with
𝔗𝔥𝔢 𝔚𝔞𝔰𝔥𝔦𝔫𝔤𝔱𝔬𝔫 𝔓𝔬𝔰𝔱

Phyllis Chasanow-Richman

Illustrations by
Roy Killeen

101 Productions
San Francisco

Cover Illustration: Roy Killeen.
Color Rendering: Sara Raffetto.
Cover Design: Lynne O'Neil.

Published by 101 Productions, 834 Mission Street,
San Francisco, California 94103.
Distributed to the book trade by
The Scribner Book Companies, New York.

Best Restaurants is the trademark of 101 Productions,
registered with the United States Patent
and Trademarks Office.

Library of Congress Cataloging in Publication Data

Chasanow-Richman, Phyllis.
  Best restaurants (& others) Washington DC & environs.

  Includes index.
  1. Restaurants, lunch rooms, etc.--Washington
(D.C.)--Directories.   2. Restaurants, lunch rooms,
etc.--Maryland--Directories.   3. Restaurants, lunch
rooms, etc.--Virginia--Directories.   I. Title.
II. Title: Best restaurants (and others) Washington DC
and environs.
TX907.C547 1985   647'.95753   85-10658
ISBN 0-89286-249-1

CONTENTS

INTRODUCTION

For two centuries a world capital, Washington in the last decade also became a restaurant capital, mainly through a rapid influx of fine French restaurants. More recently, though, Washington has declared its independence from France, as Italian, Chinese—and even American—restaurants have joined the top ranks. For perhaps the first time, the best restaurants in Washington are not necessarily French restaurants. Furthermore, in this city which changes administrations as often as every four years, major changes have shaken the restaurant scene: Five of the most influential French restaurants—Sans Souci, Le Bagatelle, Rive Gauche, Le Provencal and Chez Camille—have disappeared in a mere couple of years. And a new regime has come to power.

Thus, more than ever Washington's restaurant scene can be understood only as part of an international city rather than an almost-Southern city near the seafood-rich Chesapeake Bay. Creditable seafood restaurants are rare here, though peppered steamed crabs are one of the few truly local specialties; and Southern food is encountered so infrequently as to seem foreign. Yet one can find food from Afghanistan to Zambia, perhaps more easily than one can find traditional Maryland or Virginia cooking. Trouble spots around the world eventually become cuisine sources for Washington; while there still remain dozens of Vietnamese restaurants from the last decade, in the past few years the influx has been Lebanese, Ethiopian and Salvadorean.

And power politics is played out in Washington s restaurants. One is not *what* he eats, but *where* he eats in this city. Who dines with whom and where is a staple of Washington gossip. So, the best-known and best-respected restaurants, particularly around the White House and Capitol Hill, are crowded. Reservations are difficult to get, especially for lunch. And new restaurants open every month—as well as close every month. It would be surprising if every restaurant in this book still exists six months from this writing. And good restaurants slide downhill while inadequate restaurants discover a burst of energy and improve.

But that is what keeps restaurant critics employed.

The restaurants in this book were chosen after more than eight years of writing weekly reviews and semi-annual dining guides for *The Washington Post.* They were, in most cases, visited anonymously and several times. Visits were not announced before or after dinner; a restaurant does not know it is being reviewed until that review appears in print.

I have tried to cover the range of cuisines available in Washington, concentrating on downtown restaurants but including the best of suburban eating. In addition to the best restaurants, less-than-good restaurants were included because they are well-known or have some special feature that makes them valuable for either tourists or residents to know about. It can be as useful to know which restaurants to avoid as to know which to seek.

Even during the week, it is important to make reservations at restaurants in Washington. Busy restaurants will not hold reservations very long, so you should be accurate about the time. You are likely to get better service if you eat early than if you lunch after 1:30 or dine after 10:30. And your best chance of eating well is to order from the sheet of daily specials, for these are usually the seasonal foods or special ingredients the chef was able to obtain that day. Rockfish (the local variety of bass), Maryland crab meat and Chincoteague oysters are local seafoods to be sought, as well as softshell crabs in the summer.

In order to help you find a meal to fit your budget, restaurants are categorized as inexpensive ($), moderate ($$) and expensive ($$$). These ratings are based on the average cost of a three-course meal at dinner, without cocktails or wine, tax and tip. By ordering lightly or from the low range of the menu, a meal can cost much less in some restaurants. But tax and tip alone add about one-fourth, and ordering special dishes can rapidly escalate a bill. Prices quoted were at the time of publication, and are subject to change.

$ About $15. With an inexpensive wine, tax and tip, you should expect to spend $25 to $35 a couple.

$$ About $25. Most restaurants fall into this category. If you are cautious, you could spend as little as $40 a couple after tax and tip, but extravagance could lead to bills over $70 a couple with wine or cocktails, tax and tip.

$$$ Over $30 a person without cocktails, tax and tip. That means you should expect a full meal for two to run over $80, and often $100 or considerably more after everything is paid.

—Phyllis Chasanow-Richman

THE BEST OF THE BEST
The Best of the Best are designated by a star on their reviews.

BEST AMERICAN RESTAURANTS
Expensive
Inn at Little Washington, Virginia
Morton's of Chicago, Washington
209-1/2, Washington
Windows, Virginia

Moderate
Helen's, Washington
New Orleans Emporium, Washington
West End Cafe, Washington

Inexpensive
Florida Avenue Grill, Washington
Sholl's Cafeteria, Washington and Virginia

BEST ASIAN RESTAURANTS
Expensive
Germaine's, Washington

Moderate
China Coral, Maryland
Shezan, Washington
Szechuan, Washington
Tung Bor (for dim sum), Maryland

Inexpensive
Big Wong, Washington
Madurai, Washington

BEST FRENCH RESTAURANTS
Expensive
Jean Louis, Washington
Le Lion d'Or, Washington
Le Pavillon, Washington

Moderate
L'Auberge Chez Francois, Virginia
La Brasserie, Washington

BEST ITALIAN RESTAURANTS
Expensive
Vincenzo, Washington

Moderate
Galileo, Washington

BEST LATIN AMERICAN RESTAURANTS
Moderate
Enriqueta's, Washington
Lauriol Plaza, Washington

Inexpensive
Omega, Washington

BEST MIDDLE EASTERN RESTAURANTS
Moderate
Bacchus, Washington
Kabul West, Maryland

BEST SEAFOOD RESTAURANTS
Expensive
Vincenzo, Washington

Moderate
China Coral, Maryland
Crisfield, Maryland
New Orleans Emporium, Washington

WASHINGTON D.C.

ADAMS-MORGAN
SPAGHETTI GARDEN
Italian $

Consider moving the family out of the fast-food lane to rediscover the neighborhood restaurant—for instance, the Adams-Morgan Spaghetti Garden. By the time you finish dinner, your family is likely to know that the restaurant is run by several brothers—waiters, bartender and cook—who are from Iran by way of Israel. The brother who cooks prepares hearty home-style food: tomato sauce has chunks of tomato, pasta comes from boxes but is a good brand cooked al dente. Spaghetti with clams uses canned clams, but the garlic is properly browned so that it is mild to the taste and crisp on the tongue. Meatballs are fat, light and fluffy. Pizza is just average. But lasagna is good, its noodles light and its filling oozing cheese. Homemade ravioli are chewy with plenty of meat filling. Lots of food for the money.

ADAMS-MORGAN SPAGHETTI GARDEN, 2317 18th Street NW, Washington. Telephone: (202) 265-6665. Hours: noon–midnight Monday–Saturday; noon–11 pm Sunday. Cards: AE, MC, V. Reservations suggested. Street parking. Full bar service. Wheelchair access.

Washington: Capitol Hill, Georgetown, Upper Northwest
AMERICAN CAFE

$$

Yo can't go far in the Washington area without encountering an American Cafe these days, and the kitchen shows it. Each new branch is more splashily handsome than the one before, and this chain must have cornered the market in neon. Certainly the food is fun, with fat sandwiches on croissants and jazzy renditions of quiches brunch dishes, ice cream desserts and even soups of contemporary demeanor. A lot is good—the pub food such as salads and sandwiches particularly. But many things don't translate well to far-flung management, so the subtle elegances are best left to a restaurant with only one kitchen to supervise.

AMERICAN CAFE Capital Hill location: 227 Massachusetts Avenue NE, Washington, Telephone: (202) 547-8500. Upper Northwest location: 1300 F Street NW, Washington. Telephone: (202) 737-5153. Georgetown location: 1211 Wisconsin Avenue, Washington. Telephone: (202) 337-3606. Hours: Breakfast, Lunch, and Dinner daily. Cards: AE, CB, DC, MC, V. Reservations suggested for large parties. Street parking or nearby parking lot. Full bar service. Wheelchair access.

Washington: Georgetown
APANA
Indian

$$

When looking for a restaurant of romance, of elegance, of creative and talented cooking, a restaurant for a special occasion, Washingtonians tend to think French. And what a pity, for they should consider Apana, an Indian restaurant. It is beautiful, its dim lights and walls of Indian prints are enhanced by quiet service that has remained attentive year after year. Its most obvious flaw is the silver menus that are difficult to read in the dark, but that's a small fault. The food is seasoned with moderation. Unlike the daring curries one usually expects, there is no "tongue-searing" unless you request it. Emphasize the appetizers: fried samosas or pakoras, charcoal-grilled bits of meat. The contrasts of textures, colors and flavors are frequently surprising and tantalizing, though the best bets have often not been curries but Cornish hen with ginger and coriander, shrimp with coconut and, above all, fish. Trout or red snapper is bathed in an intensely buttery sauce perfumed with—well, cardamom, at least—and punctuated by the crunch of broccoli and almonds. A few dishes are dull. But the chutneys of sour-spicy tamarind, mint with black onion seed and pomegranate, or mango will vitalize any dish. Yogurt-based raitas will cool any curry. Don't neglect the breads; the puri is as large and puffed as a sofa pillow, the paratha pocketed with the surprise of spinach and ginger or potato.

APANA, 3066 M Street NW, Washington. Telephone: (202) 965-3040. Hours: 6 pm–11 pm Sunday–Thursday; 6 pm–midnight Friday, Saturday. Cards: AE, CB, DC, MC, V. Reservations suggested. Street parking or nearby lot. Full bar service. Wheelchair access.

APPETIZERS
Served with Imli (Tamarind) Chutney

Samosa: Small, tasty loaves of dough stuffed with sweet peas, potatoes and either spiced minced meat or cauliflower. **2.85**
Bhujia: Wholesome, fresh vegetables rolled in a spiced crust served with wedges of lemon. **2.85**
Shrimp Bhujia: A spice-crusted pastry stuffed with marinated shrimp, spiced with natural herbs. **4.25**
Husaini Tikka: Sizzling morsels of marinated lamb spiced with natural herbs. **4.25**
Mughlai Tikka: Cubes of delicate, marinated sirloin heartily seasoned with herbs and spices. **4.00**
Masala Khumbi: Fresh mushrooms sauteed in a sprite, lemon-sprinkled masala seasoning. **3.85**

ENTREES
Served with long-grain pilaf and papar

Bhuna Mutton: Squares of tender lamb pungently sauteed in cinnamon, ginger, onion and garlic. **12.00**
Tandoori Murg: A traditional Indian delicacy of seasoned spring chicken roasted Punjabi style. **9.25**
Murg Korma: Spiced spring chicken, braised in a savory sauce of youghart and shredded coconut. **9.25**
Tithar: Baked cornish hen slightly seasoned with ginger and lemon basted with coriander and cognac. **9.75**
Jhinga Kebab: Hearty jumbo shrimp speared on a skewer with onion, tomato and green pepper. **13.50**
Palak Paneer: Apana's unique savory cheese bathed in a blend of fresh spinach, cream and cumin. **8.50**
Gobhi Sabji: A vegetable dish of cauliflower and tomato, delicately spiced with ginger root and black onion seed. **8.25**
Khumbi Bhaji: Slices of mushroom and whole green peas blended in a sauce of youghart and ghee. **9.00**

Basmati Rice: A hearty, aromatic Indian rice garnished with braised onions. **3.50**
Tarka Dal: Stirred onions and lentils robustly seasoned with mustard and black onion seeds, cumin and ginger. **3.00**
Khattewalla Chola: Chick-peas and potato braised in Tamarind. **3.50**
Palak Paneer: A delectable dish of Apana's own cheese and a spiced blend of fresh spinach. **3.75**
Kheera Ka Raita: A refreshing blend of cucumber, youghart and paprika. **2.00**
Bundi Ka Raita: Delicious Basen morsels in a sauce of plain youghart and oregano. **2.00**
Pakora Ka Raita: Spice-crusted vegetables in youghart. **2.00**
Gobhi Sabji: Cauliflower and tomato spiced with ginger and mustard seeds. **3.25**
Alu Baingon: Coriander-spiced eggplant, potatoes and ripe tomatoes seasoned in black onion see. **3.25**

CHUTNEYS AND CONDIMENTS
Dhaniya Chutney: Fresh coriander with lemon juice, ginger and red pepper. **1.50**
Pudina Chutney: Fresh mint chutney seasoned with black onion seed
and pomegranate seed. **1.50**
Salad: A refreshing combination of tomato, onion, cucumber and ginger. **3.00**
Mango: Chutney. **1.50**
Mango: Achar. **1.50**
Lemon: Achar. **1.50**

BREADS
Prepared to order.
Puri: A crisp and fluffy Indian wheat bread. **1.25**
Paratha: Whole wheat flat bread warmed in ghee. **1.50**
Stuffed Paratha: Whole wheat flat bread with spiced potato stuffing. **1.75**
Palak Paratha: Whole wheat flat bread stuffed with fresh spinach
and minced ginger. **2.00**
Chapati: 1.00

DESSERTS
Kheer: A honey-sweetened rice pudding sprinkled with rosewater. **3.00**
Mango Pudding: 2.75
Ice cream: Mango, Rose, Pistachio, and Chocolate Cinnamon. **3.00**
Sherbets: by La Sorbet. **3.00**
Fresh Melon: 3.00
Gulab Jamun: 3.00
Rasmalai: 3.00

Washington: Georgetown
AU PIED DE COCHON
French

$

Au Pied de Cochon at its most crowded is probably at its most fun. Even the line at the door seems happy, for this is a watering hole as much as an eating place. Tables are inches apart, and plates have been known to pass among them to help newcomers make their choices. The waiters rush you—no wonder—and may be abrupt. They also may be witty and amusing. The food gives you a lot of calories for your money; dishes tend to be heavy and robust, served in large portions. Sauces are weighty. But it's adequate for bistro food. The best buy, when available, is lobster (also the best buy at the sibling restaurant next door, Aux Fruits de Mer). The cold pigs' feet are marvelous, if you like pigs' feet. You can order a range from omelets, quiches and crepes to London broil (rare, crusty and an enormous portion, though the sauce has its rough edges). And if you ask about the house wine, the waiter is apt to say something like, "I've had worse." In sum, the surroundings and the food are engaging and down-to-earth, as well as a good value.

AU PIED DE COCHON, 1335 Wisconsin Avenue NW, Washington. Telephone: (202) 333-5440. Hours: Open 24 hours a day, except Monday (closed 1:30 am–10 am). Cards: AE, MC V. No reservations. Street parking. Full bar service.

Washington: Georgetown
AUX FRUITS DE MER
Seafood   **$$**

There may be no salty breeze, but Aux Fruits de Mer
has all the life of a busy harbor, its small bare tables
wedged on two levels, its dark wooden walls dotted with
portholes, its window aquarium showing the automobile
lights of Wisconsin Avenue through a watery filter. For
such a hustle-bustle, late-night, quick-service place,
Aux Fruits de Mer has an extensive seafood menu: eight
or more daily seafood specials—from rockfish duglere
to fresh tuna with bearnaise—a couple of meat dishes
and a standing menu with lobster, crab and shrimp
variations, fish fillets, even bouillabaisse and cioppino.
Prices are low. Fish are cooked with reasonable care,
their sauces unassuming but pleasant. There may be a
canned mushroom here and there, but the value is
impressive. The clam chowder is homey and fresh, the
oysters briny and very low priced. Smoked salmon may
be damp and show evidence of clumsy handling, but it
makes a sufficient late-night supper with its vegetable
salad and garnish. You can skip the french fries and
coleslaw that come with the entrees, and the desserts
suffer from age and indifference.

AUX FRUITS DE MER, 1329 Wisconsin Avenue NW,
Washing on. Telephone: (202) 965-2377. Hours: 11:30
am–1:30 am Sunday–Thursday; 11:30 am–2:30 am
Friday, S turday. Cards: AE, CB, DC, MC, V. Reserva-
tions for dinner only. Street parking. Full bar service.

Washington: Downtown
BACCHUS ✽
Middle Eastern

$$

Now the dining room is more elegant and the menu somewhat expanded, and the food is as good as ever in this small Lebanese restaurant. The temptation is to order just a spread from among the appetizers—superb hummus with ground meat and pine nuts, fiery homemade sausages, phyllo-wrapped meat or spinach, fried stuffed vegetables, baba ghanouj, tabooli, kibbe—all exceptionally good versions of Middle Eastern standbys. But the main dishes are too hard to resist: chicken or lamb on crisped pita slathered with yogurt, kebabs that are carefully seasoned and cooked, seasoned rice dishes. The solution? Order a mezze—a variety of appetizers—and fill in with main dishes, or return to try the rest.

BACCHUS, 1827 Jefferson Place NW, Washington. Telephone: (202) 785-0734. Lunch: noon–2 pm Monday–Friday. Dinner: 6 pm–10 pm Monday–Thursday; 6 pm–10:30 pm Friday, Saturday. Closed Sunday. Cards: AE, MC, V. Reservations suggested. Street parking. Full bar service.

MAIN COURSES

Lahm Mechwi
(Shish Kebab)

Tender cubes of lamb specially marinated, grilled
with onions, tomatoes and mushrooms, served on a
bed of rice and garnished with almonds and pine
kernels.

Kafta Mechwi

U.S. Choice ground beef mixed with chopped onions,
parsley, herbs and spices, grilled and served on a
bed of rice, garnished with almonds and pine kernels.

Shish Taouk

Tender cubes of chicken marinated in lemon, olive
oil, garlic and fine spices, grilled. Served on a bed of
rice, garnished with almonds and pine kernels.

Sedr Djaj Mechwi

Fresh, boneless breast of chicken, specially spiced,
marinated and splashed with garlic and lemon.
Served with rice or salad.

Warak Inab Mahshi
(Grape Leaves)

Grape leaves stuffed with rice, minced meat and fine
spices, rolled and boiled in lemon juice. Served with
yogurt salad.

Malfouf Mahshi

Cabbage stuffed with rice, minced meat, garlic and
fine spices, rolled and boiled in lemon juice and
promegranate sauce. Served with yogurt or Lebanese salad.

Riz Bel Djaj

Breast of Chicken served on a bed of spiced rice,
minced meat, almonds and pine kernels. Served with
yogurt salad or house salad.

Ouzi

Lamb served on a bed of spiced rice, minced meat,
almonds and pine kernels, served with yogurt or
house salad.

Washington: Georgetown
Virginia: Alexandria
BAMIYAN
Afghan $$

The emphasis at Bamiyan is not on decoration or
service, which are both adequate, but on the food itself.
The food is a revelation to anyone who has not tasted
the cooking of Afghanistan. The best introduction is
aushak—as an appetizer, soup or main dish—the homemade noodles stuffed with leeks or scallions and sauced
with yogurt and mint with pools of tomato and meat
sauce. An unlikely combination, but a medley of genius.
For main courses, the cumin-scented kebabs, chicken or
lamb, are charcoal tinged and juicy; the stews and rice
pilafs fragrant; the spinach dishes the only disappoint-
ments. Don't ignore the side dishes, particularly pumpkin
topped with yogurt and meat sauce, as inspired a
combination as the aushak. Then cardamom tea and a
papery fried pastry. Finally gratitude for a distinctive
meal at a reasonable cost. And now you can eat Afghan
in Alexandria.

BAMIYAN Georgetown location: 3320 M Street NW,
Washington. Telephone: (202) 338-1896. Hours: 5:30
pm–11 pm daily. Cards: AE, MC, V. Reservations suggested. Street parking. Full bar service. Wheelchair
access. Non-smoking area.

Washington: Downtown
BIG WONG ✳
Chinese $

Chinatown in recent years has gone fancy and Szechuanese, but Big Wong reminds us why we were happy with Cantonese for so long. Its garish green facade and basement location lead you to appropriate expectations: the prices are very low, and the mood is hectic. What is a surprise is the breadth of the menu, with every kind of sea creature, and the myriad of Cantonese cooking methods. Lunch offers an extensive dim sum menu as well as the super-bargain luncheon specials. But go beyond to explore steamed dishes, noodle dishes, casseroles. Or see how delectable a plain old standby—stir-fried shrimp—can be when Big Wong does it as jumbo crisp and juicy crystal shrimp with walnuts.

BIG WONG, 610 H Street NW, Washington. Telephone: (202) 638-0116. Hours: 11 am–midnight daily. Cards: MC, V. Reservations suggested. Street parking. Beer only.

Washington: Georgetown
BISTRO FRANCAIS
French

$$

Over the years the Bistro Francais has matured, extended
its menu and developed some depth to its kitchen so
that while the rotisserie-cooked tarragon chicken still
remains one of the few really good roast chickens in
town, you can now also depend on this bistro for a spicy
and lavish couscous on Thursdays and an interesting
variety of daily specials which emphasize seafoods. The
dining room, poster-encrusted and with flourishes of
etched glass, is as full of energy as the waiters and the
Georgetown crowd. And the food, if not memorable,
maintains a high standard. Pale veal, rich cream sauces,
fresh vegetables and a wine list with a half-dozen
choices by the glass at reasonable prices make the
Bistro Francais a place to remember when hunger hits
in Georgetown. What's a heavy tart crust or a dull pate
here and there when a restaurant offers to feed you
decently from early morning until the middle of the
night?

BISTRO FRANCAIS, 3124–28 M Street NW, Wash-
ington. Telephone: (202) 338-3830. Hours: 11 am–3 am
Sunday–Thursday; 11 am–4 am Friday, Saturday. Cards:
AE, DC, MC, V. Reservations suggested. Street parking
or nearby lot. Full bar service. Wheelchair access.

Washington: Downtown
BREAD OVEN
French

$$

The thrill is gone at the 19th Street Bread Oven. Despite promises of a new look, recent visits showed the usual array of largely cream-sauced fish, seafoods and meats, and cooking that was all right but nothing more. A string bean and scallop salad was delicious (though overdressed), but a seafood terrine was oddly yellow and orange in spots and tasted spongy and fishy. Seafood fricassee was better, though a swamp of cream with fairly good seafoods afloat; and lamb steak could have been steamed rather than grilled for all its crustiness. Pastries were heavy-handed and suffered from Washington's summertime sogginess. Best of the visit? The waitress, whose enthusiasm was undampened by weather or wan attendance.

BREAD OVEN, 1220 19th Street NW, Washington. Telephone: (202) 466-4264. Breakfast: 7:45 am–11 am Monday–Saturday. Lunch: 11:30 am–3 pm Monday–Saturday. Dinner: 5:30 pm–10 pm Monday–Saturday. Closed Sunday. Cards: AE, CB, DC, MC, V. Reservations suggested. Street parking or nearby lot. Full bar service. Wheelchair access.

Washington: Capitol Hill
THE BROKER
Swiss   **$$**

An outpost of elegance on Barracks Row is The Broker, brick-walled and skylighted. The restaurant retains signs of its Swiss origins—fondues both cheese and chocolate, and bundnerfleish and roesti on the menu— yet fits among the new American restaurants that experiment and invent with what each season produces. Your artichoke may have been marinated in raspberry vinegar and garnished with fresh berries (not bad, but not quite a match made in heaven) or your pompano grilled with a garnish of finely diced lemon (deliciously fresh fish grilled just right and unsullied by overworked imaginations). Generally the food is good, and occasionally it soars much higher; chicken wrapped in pastry, a tough dish to carry off, is accomplished with the pastry flaky straight through and the chicken breast juicy—in fact, a little underdone. The Broker offers endearing touches: a basket of breads and giant paper-thin crackers with anchovy butter, an option of just-baked cheese bread, a wine list that is agreeable and reasonable, and homemade chocolate truffles. Chocolate fanatics are inclined to The Broker for its chocolate pate, three layers of sheer chocolate—milk, white and bittersweet— on pools of raspberry and creme anglaise.

THE BROKER, 713 8th Street SE, Washington. Telephone: (202) 546-8300. Lunch: 11:30 am–2:30 pm Monday–Friday. Dinner: 5:30 pm–10 pm Monday–Thursday; 6 pm–11 pm Friday, Saturday; 5 pm–9 pm Sunday. Cards: AE, MC, V. Reservations required. Valet parking. Full bar service. Wheelchair access. Jacket and tie required.

Washington: Downtown
CAFE SPLENDIDE
Austrian
$

Splendide may be an overstatement, but one could certainly verify Cafe Splendide as charmant. This is basically a cheery little Austrian tearoom much like one would find on the main street of an Alpine ski resort. It is easy enough to find flaws in the food here, but Cafe Splendide offers a remarkably good value for a downtown restaurant, particularly at dinner, since the menu and prices remain the same as at lunch. Perhaps the best of the food is an Austrian hamburger, highly seasoned and kneaded with green pepper, cooked very rare yet very crusty and topped with seasoned butter and a bacon strip. Other main courses—like a brochette of beef and pork tenderloin, chicken breast zingara or scallops wrapped in bacon—are satisfying food that needs a little more attention in the preparation. If you are looking for a first course or an accompaniment, turn to a salad—the salade Splendide, a crisp and bright array of watercress, apples, tomatoes, cauliflower, endive and walnuts. The bread is quite good, with a thick crust and a chewy interior, and a meal ends on a high note with a wide choice of homemade pastries of unexpectedly high quality. Cafe Splendide is a bright, friendly place for a light meal or dessert, with friendly prices and an Eastern European aura, in itself a rare thing for Dupont Circle.

CAFE SPLENDIDE, 1521 Connecticut Avenue NW, Washington. Telephone: (202) 328-1503. Hours: 9 am–11:30 pm Tuesday–Thursday; 9 am–1:30 am Friday; 8 am–1:30 am Saturday; 8 am–11:30 pm Sunday. Closed Monday. No credit cards. Reservations suggested. Street parking. Full bar service. Wheelchair access.

CANTINA D'ITALIA
Italian   **$$$**

Northern Italian restaurants come and go (and keep
coming), but all the while Cantina d'Italia remains at the
top. It is an uncompromising sort of restaurant, refusing
to make more servings of a single dish than the kitchen
finds viable, refusing to ignore the seasons and serve a
stable year-round menu, even refusing to open on
Saturday nights. Cantina serves a variety of antipasti,
mostly vegetable salads that sound simple and overpriced,
but are so fresh and ripe that they make their point. The
pastas are smooth and supple, sauced with complexities
of meat essences and vegetables and seafoods; they are
imaginative concoctions and often superb. Main dishes
are the most variable, with the best being the cold
ones—fish with homemade mayonnaise or paper-thin
marinated raw meat—as well as most seafood and veal
offerings. Duck and rabbit have heavy flavors and
textures here, sometimes veal scaloppine is overcooked,
sometimes overseasoned. But when Cantina hits the
mark, there is no more distinguished food among Italian
restaurants. Desserts are marvelous. The wine list is of
considerable depth. And the series of small rooms break
into cozy dining spaces, though the decor leans to
excess and is considerably less fresh and natural than
the food. Among the great restaurants of Washington,
Cantina d'Italia has lasted longest, never wavering from
maintaining a distinctive personality as well as high
standards.

CANTINA D'ITALIA, 1214–A 18th Street NW, Washing-
ton. Telephone: (202) 659-1830. Lunch: noon–2 pm
Monday–Friday. Dinner: 6 pm–10:30 pm Monday–
Friday. Closed Saturday, Sunday. Cards: AE, CB, DC,
MC, V. Reservations required. Street parking or nearby
parking lot. Full bar service.

Washington: Upper Northwest
CASPIAN TEA ROOM
Middle Eastern   **$$**

There is an embassy-elegant air to this shopping center tearoom. The front is clearly commercial, with a pastry case displaying a sumptuous selection of tarts and cakes grandly decorated, but in the back is a showroom of antiques even more sumptuous, gilded and inlaid and draped with velvets. In between is a dining area reflected in gilded pier mirrors and lined with flowered rose wallpaper. The service is less polished than the furniture, with long waits sometimes for food and occasional confusion over who gets what. But the food is often worth the wait. The menu is largely Persian dishes with pan-European accents. Desserts are excellently French, European dishes range from dull to fine and the Iranian dishes are invariably delicious. The kebabs are likely to be outstanding, and there is fessenjan, the chicken-pomegranate dish that is one of the great legacies of the Persian empire. At dinner, fish are good choices among the Western dishes. And eggs have been very well handled, from just-runny eggs Benedict to a nicely done, softly layered omelet. But at the Caspian Tea Room the rice is the star, accompanied by butter to moisten it, tiny bowls of tangy, spicy ground sumac to sprinkle over it and a tiny cup with a raw egg yolk to work into the mixture while the rice is steamy enough to cook it to a custardy texture. Save room for beautiful pastries–strawberry napoleons with fine flaky puff pastry, butter cream tarts that truly taste of butter, creamy

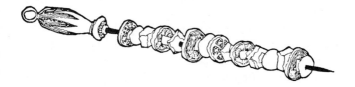

mousses in thin chocolate shells and Bavarian creams glazed with tart apricot. A little heaviness here and there doesn't interfere much with their dazzle.

CASPIAN TEA ROOM, 4801 Massachusetts Avenue NW, Washington. Telephone: (202) 244-6363. Hours: 9 am–9:30 pm Monday–Saturday. Closed Sunday. Cards: AE, CB, DC, MC, V. Reservations suggested. Street parking or nearby lot. Full bar service. Wheelchair access.

Washington: Downtown
C. F. FOLKS
American $

It may be a distinction not everyone would seek, but C. F. Folks is about the hardest restaurant to find in downtown Washington. It's just a little diner, hidden next to The Palm, but a rare diner that uses ripe tomatoes and red bell peppers in its salads, and has such daily specials as Indian mattar pannir with homemade cheese and basmatti rice, jambalaya and conch chowder. The menu features sandwiches—thick and generous, though not so ambitious as to include freshly roasted turkey, for instance. The blackboard specials are such a soft sell that you don't know until your order arrives that the burrito platter includes two huge ones, plus a giant mound of refried beans and a lovely, fresh salad. Open just for lunch, C. F. Folks serves a short menu of modestly priced food—cuisines ranging from the Middle East to the Far East—in a luncheonette raised to elegance with tablecloths and an outdoor cafe.

C.F. FOLKS, 1225 19th Street NW, Washington. Telephone: (202) 293-0162. Lunch: 11:45 am–3 pm Monday–Friday. Closed Saturday, Sunday. No credit cards. No reservations. Street parking or nearby lot. No alcoholic beverages. Wheelchair access.

FALL/WINTER
Specials

SOUP	ENTREES

MONDAY

FRENCH ONION OR MINESTRONE	LOUISIANA RED BEANS AND RICE OR CHICKEN OR SHRIMP ETOUFEE

TUESDAY

MEXICAN CORN CHOWDER OR BLACK BEANS + CHORIZO	BURRITOS OR QUESDILLAS OR ENCHILADAS OR BUDIM DE TORTILLAS

WEDNESDAY

INDIAN LENTIL OR CREAM OF BROCCOLI	DORO WAT WITH INJERA, BASMATI RICE, CHUTNEY AND PAPADUMS

THURSDAY

MUSHROOM OR SOUPE DE POISSON	STEAK SANDWICH OR OYSTER POOR BOY OR FRIED CATFISH

FRIDAY

SAFFRON CLAM CHOWDER OR CONCH CHOWDER	MIDDLE EASTERN PLATTER WITH TAHINI CREAM, EGGPLANT, KIBBEH, KOFTA OR KEBAB

TORTA RUSTICA

Charley's Crab is one of those big, brash restaurants with a heart of gold—if you don't scratch too deep. The trick is to pay attention to the catch of the day—the list of fresh fish to be poached or charcoal grilled. The king salmon can be pink velvet, the rockfish sweetly moist. The sauces—served on the side—neither add nor detract much. But Charley's is addicted to flourishes, only some of which work. Its garlicky steamed mussels are fine, but the large, creamy crab cakes could use less cream; they are not bad, but the crab is eclipsed by white sauce and seasoning. Steer clear of sauced and fried and otherwise fiddled-with seafoods. Plain, good fish in a lively bar or in a very pretty dining room that could pass for a sea captain's mansion and service that has settled into warm and efficient receptiveness make Charley's a nice place to visit.

CHARLEY'S CRAB, 1101 Connecticut Avenue NW (in the Connecticut Connection), Washington. Telephone: (202) 785-4505. Lunch: 11:30 am–3 pm Monday–Saturday. Dinner: 5 pm–10 pm Monday–Saturday. Closed Sunday. Cards: AE, CB, DC, MC, V. Reservations suggested. Full bar service. Street parking or nearby lot. Wheelchair access. Non-smoking area.

APPETIZERS

New England Clam Chowder	2.75	Seviche	5.95
Hot Curried Crabmeat Bisque	2.95	*With marinated fresh fish, cucumber, red onion, avocado and sweet red pepper*	
With a splash of sherry		Crabmeat Balls, *creamy rule sauce*	4.50
Charley's Chowder	2.25 per person	Clams Larry, *with crabmeat stuffing*	3.95
Mediterranean style fish chowder		Clams Casino, *with bacon, herbs and wine*	3.95
1/2 dozen Chilled Cherrystone Clams	4.95	Oysters Florentine, *with spinach, onion and bacon*	3.95
1/2 dozen Iced Fresh Oysters	4.95	Combination of the above three	3.95
Shrimp Cocktail	6.50	Escargot	4.95
Lump Crabmeat Cocktail	6.95	Selected Hot Hors d'Oeuvres Platter	
Chilled Raw Bar Platter	9.95	*Oyster florentine, clam larry, scallops, crabmeat balls, clam casino and frog legs*	
Oysters, clams, shrimp, smoked fish, ½ dungeness crab		Steamed Mussels, *with drawn butter and lemon*	5.50 per person
Smoked Norwegian Salmon Platter	6.95	Mussels ala Muer	4.50
With chopped egg, capers and onions, homemade bread		*Steamed in garlic butter, wine and herbs*	5.50
Sherry Buttered Cape Scallops	4.75	Mussels Provencale	6.95
Broiled and laced with sherry		*In a sauce of tomatoes, herbs and wine*	
Fried Calamari	4.95		
Squid rings lightly fried until golden, served with mustard sauce and lemon			

HOMEMADE PASTA

Red or White Clam Sauce ... 5.95 Primavera, *with sauteed fresh vegetables* ... 4.95
Fettucine Alfredo, *with cream & italian cheeses* ... 5.95

DINNER ENTREES

All entrees include hot homemade bread and your choice of a side dish

FRESH FISH OF THE DAY
BROILED, CHARGRILLED or POACHED as indicated on the daily flyer. Served with potato and vegetable garniture. Includes your choice of homemade tartar sauce, bearnaise sauce or anchovy butter.

CHARLEY'S BUCKET . 19.75 per person
In this don-east feast for ONE OR TWO, you'll find whole live Maine lobster, mussels, dungeness crab, steamers, corn on the cob and boiled redskin potatoes

CAPE SCALLOPS PRIMAVERA	14.50
Sauteed with fresh vegetables, served with rice pilaf	
SHRIMPS DANIELLE	14.95
Broiled in garlic butter, wine and herbs, served with rice pilaf	
IMPERIAL SHRIMPS ORLY	14.95
Battered and fried until golden, served with rice pilaf	
CHARLEY'S SEAFOOD PLATTER	17.50
Oyster, clams, crabcake, frog legs, shrimp orly and filet of fresh fish, served with sauteed fresh vegetables	
FRESH FILET OF FLOUNDER	
WITH CRABMEAT STUFFING, *Rice pilaf* .	13.50
BROILED CAPE SCALLOPS	15.50
Served with rice pilaf	
MARYLAND LUMP CRABMEAT CAKES	17.95
With creamy rule sauce	
SEAFOOD SAUTE	17.95
Shrimps, scallops and king crabmeat sauteed in garlic butter wine and herbs, served with rice pilaf	
ALASKAN KING CRAB LEGS	23.50
Steamed, broiled or chilled	

BOUILLABAISSE	17.95
An adapted seafood stew of Marseilles with crab, ½ Maine lobster, clams, mussels and fish blended with saffron, fennel and other aromatics	
PAELLA	18.95
Our interpretation of this Spanish classic includes ½ Maine lobster, clams, mussels, fish, chicken, sausage, mushrooms and rice simmered with saffron and other spices	

LIVE MAINE LOBSTER
Steamed or Broiled,	
1 and 2 lb. Lobsters	starting at 15.95
BAKED STUFFED LOBSTER LARRY	17.95
1 lb. Maine lobster split and stuffed with a rich blend of crabmeat, fresh mushrooms and white cream sauce, then oven broiled	
12 OZ. NEW YORK STRIP SIRLOIN	15.95
FILET MIGNON	15.95
Bearnaise or anchovy butter available for steaks	
ROAST RACK OF BABY LAMB	17.25
Marinated in herbs, served with rice pilaf	

STEAK & SEAFOOD COMBINATIONS
PETITE FILET and	
1 lb. Maine Lobster	21.95
Alaskan King Crab Legs	21.50
Shrimps Danielle	16.95

HOMEMADE PASTA

Made on the premises daily with noodles from semolina flour and tossed with freshly made sauces. Served with tossed salad and homemade bread

LITTLENECK CLAM FETTUCINE VERDE	12.50	SHRIMP AND ARTICHOKES	11.50
Steamed in a sauce of garlic and herbs		*In a rich blend of tomatoes, garlic butter and herbs*	

SEAFOOD PASTA PAGLIARA ... 12.95
With shrimp, sweet scallops, fresh spinach and mussels in a rich sauce of garlic and herbs

SALADS

Tossed Salad Greens	2.25
Spinach Seafood Salad	4.95
Charley's Caesar Salad	2.95

SIDE DISHES

Vegetable du Jour	1.50
Rice Pilaf	1.50
Boiled Redskin Potatoes	1.25
Baked Potato	1.75

Colombian Coffee ... 1.25   Orange Pekoe, Mint or Darjeeling Tea, ... 1.25   Milk ... 1.25
Freshly brewed, decaffeinated coffee ... 1.25   No Caffeine "Almond Sunset" Herb Tea ... 1.25

CHARLIE CHIANG'S
Chinese   **$$**

Clearly, Charlie Chiang's aims for a big splash. The overall look is Hong Kong extravagance, but unlike most Hong Kong restaurants, this has space between the tables, soft colors in the carpet, sun filtering through vast windows. One feels well cared for at Charlie Chiang's. One does not, however, necessarily feel well fed. While one can find a delicious meal on the long menu, it takes a good bit of ducking and weaving to avoid mediocre dishes. Appetizers, for the most part, are gummy, oversweetened or dried out, although I did find two good ones. Shrimp balls are light and fluffy, with the taste of shrimp and the crunch of water chestnuts. And crispy and sweet walnuts are a delight of crunch. Charlie Chiang's soup, too, is delicious, a slightly thickened broth with clouds of egg, bits of fish, corn, tiger lily buds and the aroma of sesame oil. The main dishes sound poetic, but little of the food is as exciting as the description and appearance promise. The lamb and pork tend to have a slippery and mushy texture, sauces are one-dimensional, lobster and shrimp have been tasteless and crispy and spicy duck stringy with fatty, limp skin. If Charlie Chiang's continues to be successful, it will be for dishes such as pork with dried bean curd, a wonderful mingling of aromas in which no one dominated. That dish and another one at lunch, General Tso's shrimp, made me wonder whether the kitchen is at its best midday.

CHARLIE CHIANG'S, 1912 I Street NW, Washington. Telephone: (202) 293-6000. Lunch: 11:30 am–3 pm Monday–Friday; noon–3 pm Saturday, Sunday. Dinner: 5 pm–10:30 pm Monday–Thursday; 5 pm–11 pm Friday, Saturday; 5 pm–11 pm Sunday. Cards: AE, CB, DC, MC, V. Reservations suggested. Valet parking at dinner. Full bar service. Wheelchair access.

Washington: Downtown
CHAUCER'S
American $$

Everyone likes to have a little-known, unexpectedly good and comfortable restaurant tucked away to call forth when the situation suggests a nice evening but not ultimate grandeur. Chaucer's is wrapped in wood paneling and carpet, with a skylight down one side. Its service is attentive and its menu creative. Best of all, it has good food—far from flawless, yet always with something special to recommend it. A special of lobster-filled homemade ravioli with curry cream at first taste lacks finesse but grows more endearing with each bite. Oysters in beurre blanc with salmon caviar is well executed. Perhaps most important to know about is the pre- and post-theater fixed-price dinner, which offers the likes of good hearty rabbit pate, soup or salad, with a choice of main dishes including a beautifully done

breast of chicken diablo, plus dessert, coffee or tea. In all, this is a fashionable little restaurant that sits neatly at the top of the second rung.

CHAUCER'S, 1733 N Street NW, Washington. Telephone: (202) 296-0665. Breakfast: 7 am–9:30 am Monday–Friday; 8 am–11 am Saturday; 8 am–10:30 am Sunday. Brunch: 11:30 am–3 pm Sunday. Lunch: 11:30 am–3 pm Monday–Friday. Dinner: 5:30 pm–11 pm Monday–Sunday. Cards: AE, CB, DC, MC, V. Reservations suggested. Free valet parking. Full bar service. Jacket suggested.

Dinner

Shrimp Pernod	13.25
Sautéed, in a White Wine Cream Sauce Seasoned with Tarragon and a Hint of Pernod	
Broiled Salmon Steak with Sauce Béarnaise	17.00
Dover Sole	17.50
Sauté Meunière	
Broiled Bay Scallops with Sesame Seeds	14.75
Warm Breast of Duck Salad	15.50
On Fresh Greens with Raspberry Vinegar	
Pan Fried Quail	14.75
With Country Ham and Pearl Onions	
London Mixed Grill	18.50
Filet Mignon, Lamb Chop, Calf's Liver, Kidney, Chicken, Bacon, Grilled Mushroom Cap, Tomato	
Loin Lamb Chops	16.50
Served with Fresh Mint Sauce	
Veal Chaucer's	15.50
Scallopine topped with Artichokes, Mushrooms, Scallions and Grated Swiss Cheese	
Roast Prime Ribs of Beef with Yorkshire Pudding	17.00
Grilled Filet Mignon with Sauce Béarnaise	17.00
Veal Chop Prince Orloff	18.50
A Grilled Loin Chop topped with Duxelles and Sauce Mornay	

Desserts

Strawberries with Sour Cream and Brown Sugar	4.00
Crème Brulée	3.00
Irish Whiskey Cake	4.00
Selection from The Pastry Cart	3.25
Homemade Ice Cream or Sorbet	3.00
Lindt Canterbury Chocolate Cake	3.25

Washington: Downtown
CHINA INN
Chinese

$

Chinese restaurants vary inscrutably from season to season, and some from day to day. But the China Inn veers startlingly within a single meal from superb to sadly deficient. It can be the best restaurant in Chinatown, then totally flop with some simple dish. Fortunately, prices are low enough to warrant a few errors, and the management is cheerful about taking back its failures. Service, above all, is solicitous in this tightly packed restaurant refurbished in Easter-basket colors. As for what to order, remember that fried foods tend to be greasy, but for appetizers like squid in a puffy yellow batter or shrimp toast, the greasiness may be worth bearing. China Inn's poached fish with ginger as julienned roots and pickled shoots is delectable, and colorfully described on the menu as "Fish Dipped in Boiling Water with Spices." And either smoked lobster or smoked crabs is definitely worth ordering; the very sweetest crustaceans are stir-fried with ginger and scallions long enough to develop a smoky flavor. In general, stick to the menu's front page, the house specialties. Inside is a long listing of Cantonese variations-

on-themes, but the standards such as beef with broccoli are the most pedestrian renditions. And even the standard stir-fries among house specialties—chef's chicken with black beans and hot peppers, or mu shi pork that is largely cabbage though appealingly crisp and tangy—are not outstanding, but merely pleasant. Concentrate on seafoods, and keep trying until China Inn produces its best for you.

CHINA INN, 629–631 H Street NW, Washington. Telephone: (202) 842-0909. Hours: 11 am–3 am Monday–Thursday; 11 am–4 am Friday, Saturday; 11 am–1:30 am Sunday. Cards: AE, MC, V. Reservations suggested. Street parking. Full bar service.

Washington: Georgetown
CLYDE'S
American $$

More of a Georgetown place to go than a restaurant, Clyde's nevertheless offers a wide choice of foods from foot-long hot dogs to prime ribs, omelets to fried chicken. Don't press your luck with the kitchen. Keep in mind that this is a pub, and order pub food. The atrium and the omelet room are lovely places to eat, and the service is well meaning, though it gets lost in the crush of a crowded evening. Clyde's is at its best at breakfast or brunch, when everything served is light, fresh, pretty and unhurried.

CLYDE'S, 3236 N Street NW, Washington. Telephone: (202) 333-9180. Hours: 7:30 am–2 am Monday–Thursday; 7:30 am–3 am Friday; 9 am–3 am Saturday; 9 am–2 am Sunday. Brunch: 9 am–4 pm Saturday, Sunday. Omelet Room: 7:30 am–3:30 pm Monday–Friday; 9 am–3:30 pm Saturday, Sunday. Cards: AE, DC, MC, V. Reservations suggested. Street parking or nearby lot. Full bar service. Wheelchair access.

OMELETTES

All omelettes 5.75

Normandy
An herb omelette with sauteed mushrooms, filled with herb cheese

Clyde's
Bacon and Spinach topped with Hollandaise Sauce

Our Famous Chili Omelette
Baked with sharp cheddar cheese and onions

Florentine
Spinach with parmesan or sour cream and chives

Lorraine
Bacon or ham with cheddar or Gruyere cheese

Bonne Femme
Bacon, sauteed potatoes and onions with sour cream and chives

---

Served until 1 A.M.

Quiche	**6.50**
Lorraine or Spinach	
Eggs Benedict	**6.25**

· PASTA ·

Fettuccini Alfredo	**8.25**
Noodles tossed in sweet butter in a light cream sauce	
Fettuccini Primavera	**8.25**
Noodles sauteed in garlic butter with fresh garden vegetables in a cream sauce	
Fettuccini with Scallops	**10.50**
Noodles tossed with tender Bay Scallops in a dill cream sauce	
Tortellini	**8.25**
Meat filled pasta twists in a cream sauce or with Marinara	

... all pasta dishes may be split as an appetizer ...

APPETIZERS

Homemade Herb Cheese	**3.50**
In a crock. Served with French Bread	
Hot Wheel of Brie	**5.25**
Covered with toasted almonds and melted butter. Served with French bread	
Shrimp Cocktail	**5.95**
Rock Shrimp *(by the dozen)*	**5.95**
Broiled in garlic butter	
Steak Tartare *(5 Ozs.)*	**4.95**
(Not Available Sunday)	

DINNERS

Served 5:00 to 12:00

Steak Tartare	**8.50**
(Not Available Sunday)	
London Broil	**9.50**
Topped with mushroom gravy. Served with a vegetable and fried or baked potato	
New York Sirloin Strip Steak *(12 Ozs.)*	**14.95**
Served with a vegetable and fried or baked potato	
Beer Batter Shrimp	**9.95**
With orange mustard sauce, coleslaw and fried potatoes	
Crabcake Dinner	**9.95**
Served with coleslaw and fried potatoes	

From the Broiler	**9.95**
Bay Scallops	
Rock Shrimp (in garlic butter)	
Filet Mignon (5 ozs.)	
Choice of any two	**14.95**

Served with coleslaw and fried or baked potato

DANCING CRAB
Seafood   **$$**

In this handmade, down-home rustic setting you can celebrate the fact that Chesapeake Bay is only down the road a piece. Hammer at peppery steamed crabs on tablecloths of brown paper. Feast on all-you-can-eat specials of raw oysters and clams, spiced shrimp and steamed clams. Or eat nicely fried fillets of rockfish. But pass up anything more ambitious, such as stuffed shrimp. And don't expect much from the french fries or desserts. It is a shirt-sleeves, beer-and-crab place.

DANCING CRAB, 4611 Wisconsin Avenue NW, Washington. Telephone: (202) 244-1882. Hours: 11 am–11 pm Monday–Thursday; 11 am–midnight Friday, Saturday; 3 pm–11 pm Sunday. Cards: AE, CB, DC, MC, V. Reservations accepted up to 7:30 pm. Street parking. Full bar service. Wheelchair access.

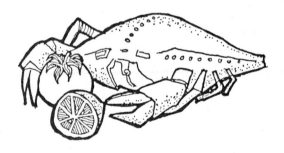

DOMINIQUE'S
French   **$$$**

Dominique's has everything. Of course, you may not
want to have everything when that includes ostrich and
rattlesnake. But that gives you an idea of why the menu
weighs as much as your briefcase and what kind of
atmosphere to expect: unbent elegance. This is a huge
circus of a restaurant where the turnover is fast, the
service breezy and friendly as well as expert. There is
always something going on, from a pre-theater bargain
of a fixed-price dinner to a Bastille Day party. Dominique
raises his own quail and mallard ducks, but his kitchen
has been known to overcook and oversauce them. He
also gives you the choice of *live* trout (ask for it au bleu)
or *fresh* trout, though not still swimming. The fish can be
wonderful; try them sauteed with scallops and julienned
vegetables. Seafoods in general are best bets, starting
with the crab soup. Ask advice. If the staff love the
mousse de foie, you probably will, too. But be wary of
anything fanciful at least until dessert, when, instead of
the unexciting pastries, you should go all out for
Elizabeth Taylor's favorite, chocolate truffles drowned
in whipped cream and almonds. Sounds horrendous,
looks disgustingly rich, tastes irresistible.

DOMINIQUE'S, 1900 Pennsylvania Avenue NW,
Washington. Telephone: (202) 452-1126. Lunch: 11:30
am–2:30 pm Monday–Friday. Dinner: 5:30 pm–midnight
Monday–Thursday; 5:30 pm–1 am Friday, Saturday.
Closed Sunday. Cards: AE, CB, DC, MC, V. Reservations
suggested. Valet parking for dinner only. Full bar
service. Wheelchair access.

Dona Flor, like its namesake in *Dona Flor and Her Two Husbands,* is from Bahia, the state of Brazil best known for its food. The chef is also Bahian and uses the palm oil (dende) and coconut milk crucial to Bahian cooking. And on a busy night the restaurant has the lilt and friendliness associated with that countryside. It helps if you start with caipirinha, the powerful drink made from Brazilian firewater called cachaca. To follow, there are dishes for the timid and dishes for the adventurous, peasant and elegant dishes, mediocre and delicious ones. Two appetizers stand out, though each is flawed. Clams a Baiana are a large portion of clams steamed in their shells with a peppery coconut broth pungent from green pepper, olive oil and herbs. Quite different is combinacao do chef, a mixed hors d'oeuvre plate. Among main dishes, my favorite is frango a passarinho, a chicken long marinated and cut into bite-size pieces (with the bone), then fried so the skin is crackly crisp and the meat is juicy and aromatic. Vatapa is also quite good, the tenderly cooked fish and shrimp, tinged red from the palm oil, in a mild and creamy coconut sauce. Shrimp are fat and juicy at Dona Flor, fish stews are carefully cooked, but lobster tails are frozen. Chicken is baked, broiled or stewed with coconut milk, as well as fried, and red meats are grilled on skewers with garlic or broiled, served crusty and often accompanied with a tomato-pepper-vinegar sauce. The feijoada is pretty good, and there is a related dish called Brazil 2001, a platter rather than a casserole, with pan-crisped collard greens as garnish. In general, Dona Flor has good, hearty food that doesn't threaten greatness. The wine list is short and includes a couple of Portuguese wines, and there is good Brazilian beer. And that's it, except for one lone dessert, which is a pale and not very tasty coconut custard, and good strong Brazilian coffee.

DONA FLOR, 4615 41st Street, Washington. Telephone: (202) 537-0404. Hours: 11:30 am–11:30 pm Monday–Friday; 5 pm–midnight Saturday; 1 pm–midnight Sunday. Cards: AE, CB, DC, MC, V. Reservations suggested. Street parking or nearby lot. Full bar service.

Washington: Downtown
DUKE ZEIBERT'S
American $$$

Once upon a time you could hardly find a good piece of plain, fresh fish in a Washington restaurant, and a thick steak was almost as rare as a rare steak. But there was Duke's, for reliable, solid, high quality plain fare. Nowadays Duke's is a vast, handsome second-floor dining room overlooking Connecticut Avenue rather than a garish eating hall, but the food is much the same: solid and unexciting, unless you consider a good piece of fish or prime-quality roast beef hash exciting. What's changed is that Washington's restaurants in general have improved, so a fine fish fillet is available many places, and even better steaks can be had than those at Duke's. Still, the restaurant has its jock-politico-celebrity ambiance, its chicken-in-the-pot and chopped-liver Old Worldliness and Duke himself. You can get a good crab cake at Duke's, homey mashed potatoes, matzo ball soup and real dill pickles. And if your idea of greatness refers to size, your dinner at Duke's will satisfy it.

DUKE ZEIBERT'S, 1050 Connecticut Avenue NW, Washington. Telephone: (202) 466-3730. Hours: 11:30 am–11:30 pm Monday–Saturday; 5 pm–10 pm Sunday. Cards: AE, DC, MC, V. Reservations suggested. Valet parking. Wheelchair access.

EL BODEGON
Spanish $$

Some restaurants could get by on their personality alone if they had to. El Bodegon does not have to, but it is a restaurant with an enthusiastic greeting, well-costumed dining rooms and flamenco dancers to accompany your paella. The owner-host comes by to pour a stream of wine down your throat. Singing "Happy Birthday" is a major production complete with flaming flan. And, not just because the rooms are crowded and the tables close, conversations cross tables along with samples of food on occasion. The food is Spanish with a high proportion of beefsteaks. The hearty soup, caldo gallego, is smoky with ham, thick with beans and leafy greens, a near-meal at a bargain price. Cold mussels in chunky vinaigrette are a light start, and a better choice than empanadas. Among the main dishes, squid is excellent—stuffed with ham and accented with wine and garlic. Paella is well laced with seafood, its rice infused with briny flavor. Veal is pale, tender, brightened with peppers and the like. Chicken is even more lively, with chunks of chorizo and ham and potato slices to soak up its sherried brown sauce. The food is strong and hearty, likable. Sangria goes well, being only minimally sweetened. For dessert there is a refreshing pineapple mousse. The menu lists more—a half-dozen main courses. And such festivity at such moderate prices suggests finding more opportunities to sample them.

EL BODEGON, 1637 R Street NW, Washington. Telephone: (202) 667-1710. Lunch: noon–2:30 pm Monday–Saturday. Dinner: 5:30 pm–10:30 pm Monday–Saturday. Closed Sunday. Cards: AE, DC, MC, V. Reservations suggested. Valet parking. Full bar service.

Carnes y aves

Tournedos salsa Madeira   15.50
Two generous beef tenderloin steaks broiled to order,
served with our chef's special Madeira sauce, and
garnished with broccoli spears, carrots and
creamed potatoes

Banderillas Manolete   12.95
Marinated beef tenderloin, smoked ham, fresh
tomatoes, peppers and onions, gently broiled on a skewer

Medallones con alcachofas salteadas   13.95
Three mini-filet mignon steaks, tastily sauteed to order
and served with Spanish artichokes in a delicate
ham sauce

Escalopes de ternera al limón   12.75
Tender veal steaks sauteed gently in a lemon butter
sauce and served with fresh garden vegetables

Pescados y mariscos

Merluza a la vasca   13.25
Fresh northern hake, shrimp and mussels, gently
simmered in a savory wine and herb sauce,
garnished with white asparagus

Lenguado relleno con cangrejo   13.95
Fresh Chesapeake Bay flounder, stuffed with
crab meat and slowly baked in a white wine
and herb sauce

Calamares rellenos en su tinta   10.75
Tender squid stuffed with ham, egg and spices
and baked in its own smoky ink and red
wine sauce

Coquilla de mariscos   11.75
Fresh shrimp and scallops lightly sauteed
with mushrooms and brandy, broiled to a golden
brown with our chef's special sauce

Washington: Georgetown and Downtown
EL CARIBE
Latin American $$

Unlike most expanding restaurants, the tiny El Caribe has opened a second branch yet maintained the high level of the first. Both branches are attractively decorated to look distinctively Latin American. The menus are similar, though the Georgetown branch is priced slightly higher to accommodate its higher rent. The Columbia Road branch is smaller, closer, more crowded; it's impossible to hold a conversation there when the guitarist is playing (though he is entertaining). At both branches, waiters respond to the hectic pace by becoming increasingly brusque, though they can also be charming and solicitous. It is hard to get past the appetizers: the shrimp afloat in garlic sauce look puny but taste wonderful, the fried squid are light and crisp, the ceviche is pleasantly pungent, and the empanadas are savory. Main dishes come with mountains of black beans and rice, very well prepared. Main dishes are samplings from Spain and several Latin American countries. Bolivia can be proud of El Caribe's sweet and tangy tongue, Spain of its squid stuffed with ham and seafood. Hefty stews of pork with bananas and root vegetables, or rabbit in wine sauce are interesting intertwinings of fragrances and textures. And the restaurants themselves are a satisfying blend of stylish surroundings and personable food at moderate prices.

EL CARIBE Georgetown location: 3288 M Street NW, Washington. Telephone: (202) 338-3121. Hours: 11:30 am–11 pm Sunday–Thursday; 11:30 am–11:30 pm Friday, Saturday. Cards: AE, CB, DC, MC, V. Reservations suggested. Free parking in rear. Full bar service. Downtown location: 1828 Columbia Road NW, Washington. Telephone: (202) 234-6969. Hours: 11:30 am–11 pm Monday–Thursday; 11:30 am–11:30 pm Friday; 1

pm–11:30 pm Saturday; 1 pm–11 pm Sunday. Cards: AE, CB, DC, MC, V. Reservations suggested. Street parking. Full bar service. Wheelchair access.

Washington: Georgetown
ENRIQUETA'S ✻
Mexican
$$$

If you still think Mexican food begins with tacos and ends with sopapillas, you have yet to discover Enriqueta's, where the cooking is Mex-Mex, not Tex-Mex. That means alternations of delicacy, subtlety and fresh crunch with pepper blaze, and a menu of such variety that it goes on for pages. Start with mussels, particularly if they are baked in a chili or mustard sauce, both irresistible. The corn-wrapped dishes—tacos, enchiladas and tamales—have a handmade character and individuality. Shrimps can be superb, sauced with a wide variety of seasonings from coriander to olives. And check out the daily specials, particularly the changing array of stuffed peppers. Enriqueta's dark and fiery mole or tangy and fiery salsa verde can be had on chicken or enchiladas. And though a few dishes sink into dullness—a shrimp ceviche, which is a lovely fresh seafood salad but lacks the pungency of proper ceviche, or "fresh" fruit drinks that are woefully watered down—Enriqueta's usually maintains a culinary sparkle that keeps its fans filling the colorful dining room's elbow-to-elbow tables. It has all the serenity of a bullfight, but also reproduces its festivity.

ENRIQUETA'S, 2811 M Street NW, Washington. Telephone: (202) 338-7772. Lunch: 11:30 am–2:30 pm Monday–Friday. Dinner: 5 pm–10 pm Sunday–Friday; 5 pm–11 pm Saturday. Cards: AE, CB, DC, MC. Reservations suggested. Street parking or nearby lot. Full bar service. Wheelchair access. Non-smoking area.

Fio's is a period piece, a representation of the 1950s, from the curved pink Formica counter that snakes through its center to the prices. On a Saturday night, Fio's has the ambience of a Greyhound bus station in full dress. One corner is sectioned off by ornate metal fencing and turned into a Mediterranean nook by a pastel mural. Around this island is a sea of tables with burgundy vinyl cloths set with assorted candles dripping free-form sculptures onto their holders. A juke box alternates the Platters and Mario Lanza. Here is the mythically correct setting for pizza of heroic quality, homemade pastas of unsung glory. The myth is completed by the peasant prices. Most of the menu consists of a recitation of daily specials. Head first for the pastas, the full range of standards, some fashioned from homemade noodles and priced at half of most restaurants' levels. This is assertive southern Italian food, and the tomato sauces are the best of the kitchen. Don't waste your visit on cream sauces or the likes of fettuccine Alfredo. The yeasty, chewy pizza has the earthiness of good bread, topped with a light wash of tomato chunks and cheese, plenty of herbs and olive oil. The full range of veal dishes is listed, though not always available and not always up to par; but the specials deserve special attention, along with the memorable oiled and garlicked vegetables that accompany them. Service is slow and sometimes confused. Fio's serves food with no pretense of refinement or delicacy, and when it is too busy the kitchen shows it. But the food is hearty and home style, and the light touch is where it counts—in the pricing.

FIO'S, 3636 16th Street NW, Washington. Telephone: (202) 667-3040. Dinner: 5 pm–11 pm Tuesday–Sunday. Closed Monday. Cards: AE, CB, DC, MC, V. Reservations suggested for parties over six. Underground parking garage. Full bar service. Wheelchair access.

ANTIPASTI

ANTIPASTO	2.00
MELONE AND PROSCIUTTO	2.00
COMBINATION SALAD	1.25
PIZZA BIANCA (White Pizza) .... Small 3.00 Large	4.00
With Cheese (small) 3.75 With Cheese (large)	5.00
ZUPPA DEL GIORNO	1.25

PASTA

LASAGNA	4.50
MANICOTTI WITH BRACIOLA	4.50
(cheese-filled pasta, stuffed pork)	
CANNELLONI	4.00
(meat-filled pasta)	
RAVIOLI WITH MEAT	4.00
RAVIOLI WITH CHEESE	4.00
TORTELLINI WITH BUTTER OR MEAT SAUCE	4.00
(meat-stuffed pasta rings)	
GNOCCHI	4.00
(potato dumplings)	
FETTUCCINE WITH MEAT SAUCE	4.50
CAVATELLI	5.50
(cheese-based dumplings)	
BUCATINI ALLA CARBONARA	6.00
(pasta with prosciutto, onions, egg and cheese)	
SPAGHETTI WITH MEATBALL	4.00
SPAGHETTI	3.50
(with meat sauce, marinara, or aglio and olio).	
LINGUINE	4.00
(with meat sauce, marinara, or aglio and olio.)	
STUFFED SHELLS	5.50
(with cheeses)	

PESCE

CLAMS	7.00
(with Linguine White or Red Sauce)	
MUSSELS	5.00
(with Linguine White or Red Sauce)	
SHRIMP MARINARA*	7.00
(meatless tomato sauce)	
SHRIMP SHERRY*	7.00
SEAFOOD PLATTER	7.00
(White or Red Sauce, clams, mussels, shrimp, king crab, squid)	
Served with Spaghetti or Salad or Peppers and Mushrooms	

THE FISHERY
Seafood   **$$**

Context is crucial to The Fishery. In the broader
context, it is one of the few seafood restaurants within a
25-mile radius that serves reliably fresh fish consistently
cooked with care. In the narrower context, the prices are
hefty for a no-tablecloth, no-reservations, few-frills
dining environment that looks like a nautical pub rather
than a setting for an expensive dinner. So, while the
prices are high, they are still better value than seafood
dinners at two-thirds the price that border on the
inedible—a frequent phenomenon in Washington. Skip
the clam chowder and the overpriced crab cakes made
of shredded crab meat. But the oysters taste as fresh as
if the seafood market were next door—which it is. The
wine list is as thoughtful and reasonable as if the owner
had his own wine shop—which he does. Rely on the
broiled fresh fish fillets and on the crab meat, with
either imperial or Norfolk stuffing. Fried shrimp and
oysters are light battered and successfully fried—no
mean feat. That's about it: broiled fish, fried seafoods,
crab-stuffed fish or shrimp, lobster and Norfolk dishes,
plus more complex specials—mousses, phyllo turn-
overs—which can be excellent. A good tangy salad
dressing and properly baked potato or some uneven
cottage fries complete the meal. Very good fish, properly
cooked, left alone to speak for itself—that's the best of
The Fishery.

THE FISHERY, 5511 Connecticut Avenue NW, Wash-
ington. Telephone: (202) 363-2144. Lunch. 11:30 am–4
pm Monday–Saturday. Dinner: 4 pm–11 pm Monday–
Sunday. Cards: AE, CB, DC, MC V Reservations
suggested. Free parking lot next door. Full bar service.
Wheelchair access.

Dinner...

Appetizers

Clam Chowder - creamy Boston style or
Maryland Crab Soup - spicy with tomatoes
    vegetables and lump crabmeat   Cup $1.95   Bowl $2.50

Oysters on the Half Shell (6) $4.50

Clams on the Half Shell $4.50 or steamed $5.50

Jumbo Shrimp Cocktail $6.50

Mussels Marinere - steamed with herbs,
    garlic, white wine and butter $5.95

Clams Casino $5.95

Crabmeat and Feta Turnovers - lump crabmeat
    and feta cheese wrapped in phylo
    triangles topped with sesame seeds $4.95

Seafood Platters

Norfolk Style (sauteed in butter)
    your choice of lump crabmeat, shrimp,
    or bay scallops   alone $13.95
                or any combination $14.95

Jumbo Fried Shrimp $13.95

Combination Platter - crabcake, shrimp
    fish, scallops, and oysters $15.95

Crabcakes - all lump crabmeat $14.95

Jumbo Stuffed Shrimp $14.95

Baked Imperial Crab - the Best in D.C. $14.50

Fried Oysters or Clams $10.95

Deep Sea Scallop Platter $12.95

Shrimp Parmesan - topped with mozzarella
    marinara sauce and linguine $12.95

Children's Platter - fish or shrimp $8.95

Maine Lobster $12.00 lb.

Fishery Salad - choice of Bleu Cheese,
    French or House dressing $1.50

Washington: Downtown
FLORIDA AVENUE GRILL ✱
American (Southern)

$

You won't find the Florida Avenue Grill listed in the phone book, because it has all the word-of-mouth publicity it needs. This keeps its few tables and long counter busy from early morning to closing time. The grill is an old-fashioned diner with Southern food served in enormous portions. You can get a mountain of pan-fried chicken or ham hocks or spareribs or meat loaf shored up with two mountains of vegetables—cooked greens or cabbage, sweet potatoes or potato salad, beans or rice. Despite a tendency to oversweeten the salads and barbecue sauces, the food is very good, seasoned heartily with black pepper. The corn muffins—crunchy with white cornmeal—are even better. And breakfast, with grits, scrapple, home fries and hot biscuits, is rib sticking. For a light snack you can get a quarter of a fried chicken between two slices of bread. The place is a favorite with Howard University medical students, taxi drivers (who may respond to your announced destination with, "So the word is out!") and whoever has managed to find the place once. Cornbread like that doesn't happen too often in a lifetime.

FLORIDA AVENUE GRILL, 1100 Florida Avenue NW, Washington. Telephone: (202) 265-1586. Hours: 6 am–9 pm Monday–Saturday. Breakfast: 6 am–1:30 pm Monday–Saturday. Closed Sunday. No credit cards. No reservations. Adjacent free parking lot. No alcoholic beverages.

DINNER MENU

SHORTRIBS of BEEF 5.95
BAR-B-QUE SPARE RIBS 5.75
TWO PORK CHOPS 4.85
ONE PORK CHOP 3.50
PAN FRIED CHICKEN.................................... 4.50
HAMBURGER STEAK.................................... 3.95
TWO HAM HOCKS...................................... 4.65
CHITTERLINGS... 4.95
MEAT LOAF 3.95
BEEF LIVER and ONIONS 3.95
FRESH PAN FRIED FISH (Friday Only).................... 4.25
TWO PIG FEET 4.50
BAKED CHICKEN (with Cornbread Dressing) 4.95

ALL DINNERS served with two vegetables.

VEGETABLES

Fresh Collard Greens   Mashed Potatoes
Baked Macaroni with Cheese   Fresh Cabbage
Candied Sweet Potatoes   Pickled Beets
Potato Salad   Rice
Garden Peas   String Beans

Vegetable — 1.10 each
Vegetable Plate (3) — 3.00   Bowl Beans — 1.25

DRINKS

Juices 45   Orange Juice/No Ice ...... .65
Soft Drinks 60   Coffee · Large .... .55
Milk · Pint...............65   Hot Chocolate · Sm....... .40
Milk · ½ Pint 45   Hot Chocolate · Lg .... .55
Coffee · Small 40   Iced Tea .... .75

DESSERT

Homemade Peach Cobbler - .95   Assorted Pies - .85

ALL SIDE ORDERS 1.10
– Carry Out Boxes .10 Extra –

FOGGY BOTTOM CAFE
American   **$$**

Not all arts thrive in Foggy Bottom. Theater, music and dance, yes. Cuisine, hardly. Foggy Bottom Cafe is therefore more than an asset. It is a necessity, an oasis. Small, noisy, casual, lively and very stylish, the Foggy Bottom Cafe can rush you to the theater with a good hamburger under your belt, or treat you after the theater to a light seafood salad or a rich calf's liver in watercress-mustard sauce or lamb chops grilled with garlic and cassis. The food is fashionable—pesto and sesame noodles and eggs Benedict. And prettily served. Usually quite good, too. The very popular shrimp and broccoli tempura, a main dish for one or appetizer for two, is greasy and served with insipid sauces, but the shrimp themselves are excellent, the broccoli still spunky. Thus, along with misses like a seafood brochette with a bitter aftertaste, there are always even more hits, and desserts are worth curtain calls.

FOGGY BOTTOM CAFE, 924 25 th Street NW (in the River Inn), Washington. Telephone: (202) 338-8707. Breakfast: 7 am–10 am Monday–Friday; 8 am–10 am Saturday, Sunday. Brunch: 10 am–2:30 pm Saturday, Sunday. Lunch: 11:30 am–2:30 pm Monday–Friday. Dinner: 5 pm–11:30 pm Tuesday–Saturday; 5 pm–10:30 pm Sunday, Monday. Cards: AE, CB, DC, MC, V. Reservations suggested. Street parking. Full bar service.

foggy bottom entrees

**veal scallopini layered with fresh
mushrooms and mozzarella cheese**
served with fresh vegetable   12.95

calf's liver with watercress-mustard sauce   8.95

shrimp and vegetable tempura
with mustard-beer and sweet and sour sauce 9.95

fresh trout with walnuts and oregano   10.95

tennessee pepper steak
marinated with bourbon and cracked peppercorns   12.95

linguini river inn
*tossed with sauteed sausage in a
light tomato and cream sauce*   11.95

honey-barbecued spareribs
half rack 7.95   *full rack*   13.95

skewers of ginger-barbecued shrimp
served over red pepper rice 12.95

duck grilled with cassis and crushed juniper   10.95

fillet steak with whole grilled mushrooms
served with vegetable and bearnaise sauce 14.95

fresh seafood sampler:
changing daily, please inquire

lamb chops grilled with tarragon butter
(2) 9.95   (3) 12.95   (4) 14.95

Washington: Georgetown
FOUR SEASONS HOTEL:
AUX BEAUX CHAMPS
French $$$

Aux Beaux Champs has built-in assets: spaciousness, subdued luxury in its table appointments and furnishings—all the benefits of a grand hotel. Its kitchen stocks the best, from truffles to foie gras to a wine list as comprehensive, particularly in its California selections, as several ordinary restaurants combined. Its menu is intriguing: rhubarb compote with the pate, lobster ravioli in corn soup, walnut cream on the chicken. Execution sometimes leaves you wishing the kitchen were not diverted—is it banquets? room service?—for the sweetbread mousse might be rubbery, the sauce not reduced to full strength, braised endive watery as it dilutes everything on the plate. Flaws like these disrupt the beauty of the meal, though the lamb noisettes may still be perfectly cooked and glistening in brown mint sauce, or homemade noodles may be exquisitely thin and cooked precisely. All is handsome, down to the lavish pastries. But sometimes beauty is only skin deep.

FOUR SEASONS HOTEL: AUX BEAUX CHAMPS, 2800 Pennsylvania Avenue NW, Washington. Telephone: (202) 342-0810. Breakfast: 7 am–11 am Monday–Friday; 8 am–11 am Saturday, Sunday. Brunch: 10 am–2:30 pm Saturday, Sunday. Lunch: noon–2:30 pm Monday–Friday. Dinner: 6:30 pm–10:30 pm daily. Cards: AE, CB, DC, MC, V. Reservations required. Valet parking. Full bar service. Wheelchair access.

Washington: Downtown
FOUR WAYS
French

$$$

This is a grand mansion, and the food should follow suit. Too often, though, what arrived on the plate in the past was more grand than delicious. Now, however, a new leaf is being turned with a chef from London's Dorchester Hotel. Early tastings show promise of culinary beauty, though not yet distinction in the taste. In the meantime, the wine list remains a strength, and the handsome rooms encourage giving Four Ways another chance.

FOUR WAYS, 1701 20th Street NW, Washington. Telephone: (202) 483-3200. Brunch: 11:30 am–3 pm Sunday. Lunch: noon–2:30 pm Monday–Friday. Dinner: 6 pm–10:30 pm Monday–Sunday. Cards: AE, CB, DC, MC, V. Reservations suggested. Valet parking. Full bar service. Jacket and tie required.

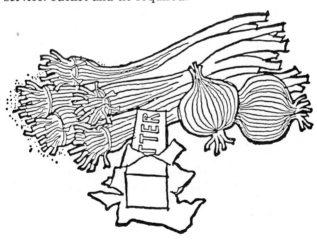

F. SCOTT'S
Continental   **$$**

Everybody waiting in line to get in on Saturday night
can tell you that F. Scott's is a good place to dine, dance,
drink, meander. It is the city's best grown-up ice cream
parlor, only here the ice cream is alcohol-laced and
served with a straw. F. Scott's has tiny tables, close
together, a champagne party atmosphere where black
tie would not be out of place. It takes only moments to
feel like a movie extra. You sip pretty pink things in
stemmed glasses, a perfumed frozen slush called ice
palace, or an antique-satin cream called toasted almond.
Small drinks they are, but they taste as if they were
designed by Busby Berkeley. Here is a menu aimed at
late-night snacking, with twice as many appetizers as
main dishes. For light eating, order the oysters and
clams by the piece or a platter of three decent-to-good
pates. The fettuccine, agnolotti and tortellini (all home-
made by a talented behind-the-scenes bit player) are
cooked al dente and tossed in rich creamy sauce, and
the steak tartare is pretty good. No wonder it is a hit
show. The food, if not worthy of awards, plays a good
supporting role to a glamorous stage set.

F. SCOTT'S, 1232 36th Street NW, Washington. Tele-
phone: (202) 965-1789. Hours: 6:30 pm–2 am Sunday–
Thursday; 6:30 pm–3 am Friday, Saturday. Cards: AE,
CB, DC, MC, V. Reservations suggested. Free valet
parking. Full bar service. Wheelchair access. Jacket
required.

LE MENU

Soups

Vichyssoise	$3.00
French Onion Soup	$3.50
Parisienne Soup	$3.50
Gazpacho Andaluz	$3.00
Chilled Cream of Cauliflower and Watercress Soup	$3.50

Savories

Jumbo Shrimp Cocktail	$7.25
Crabmeat Cocktail	$7.50
Oysters on the Half Shell ...... each	$1.00
Cherrystone Clams .... each	$1.00
Raw Bar Platter	$7.75
Oysters au Gratin .... each	$1.10
Norwegian Imported Smoked Salmon	$8.25
Smoked Trout	$5.25
Escargots de Bourgogne	$6.75
Paté Maison .... Cold $5.25 Hot	$6.25
French Brie	$4.75
Imported Smoked Ham with Melon	$5.25
Sauteed Chicken Livers (plain or garlic)	$5.95
Barbecued Miniature Drumsticks	$4.75
Crock of Herb Cheese	$3.25
Artichoke Vinaigrette	$4.95
Beluga #1 Caviar	$35.00

Salad

House Salad	$3.75
Tomato Salad	$3.25
Spinach Salad	$4.25
Paradise Salad	$4.95
Caesar Salad	$4.95
Duck Salad	$7.50
Ratatouille Salad	$4.50

Pasta

Fettuccine	$8.75
Agnolotti à la Crema	$9.75
Tortellini au Gratin	$9.50
Tortellini with Scallops and Broccoli Fleurets	$15.50
Linguine al Pesto	$8.95

Light Fare

Omelets	$8.25
Eggs Benedict	$9.25
Tidbits of Beef Tenderloin	$9.50
Steak Tartar	$9.50
Eggplant Parmigiana	$11.00

Entrées

Escaloppes of Red Snapper
With Tarragon and Dill
$17.00

Broiled Swordfish
$15.00

Filet of Sole Meuniere
$15.00

Shrimp Corsini
$15.95

Broiled Lobster
Market Price

•

Chicken Parisienne
$15.00

Roast Duck
In Orange Sauce
$15.50

•

Veal Escaloppes
With Morels
$18.50

Veal Italienne
$16.50

•

Roast Rack of Lamb
$21.00

•

Prime New York Sirloin
$19.25

New York Pepper Steak
$19.75

Filet Mignon
$19.50

Steak Diane
$19.75

Steak Maitre d'
$17.00

Tournedos Black and White
$19.75

Washington: Downtown
GALILEO ✽
Italian
$$

The room is simple, with only some greenery and pretty watercolors against the rough-textured white walls and a warren of tables cleverly placed so that the small space still allows a sense of privacy. The most prominent decoration bodes well for dinner to come: Long slim homemade bread sticks serve as centerpieces in their baskets. The menu is a handwritten array of appetizers, soups, pastas and main dishes which change twice a day. The wine list also changes with the menu, and is both modestly priced and knowledgeably chosen. In my experience there are few chances to go wrong. Such appetizers as a mixed plate of infant eggplants, tiny fresh artichokes, roasted red and yellow peppers and mushrooms compete with marinated artichokes Roman-style, or prosciutto with figs, or fried squid, or polenta with bagna cauda. Pastas escape the routine as in few other Italian restaurants: agnolotti with beets, risotto with porcini mushrooms or pumpkin puree. The thin and supple homemade noodles might be tossed with gorgonzola, tomato or wild mushrooms, or pastas might be combined with crab meat or with salami and prosciutto. As for main dishes, Cornish hen baked whole (wrapped in leaves and buried in rock salt) has the most succulent and subtle taste that bird could acquire. Loin of lamb roasted with rosemary crusty and rare, sliced thin and fanned out around a slice of kidney has been delicious, as has bollito misto arranged with baby carrots, tiny squash and a skewer of those extravagant mustard fruits which look like jewels. Large shrimp are grilled with their shells, infused with herbed oil and smokily crusty. Even plain grilled swordfish is well crusted, juicy and sea fresh. I could wish for less noise at Galileo, or for a dish to be improved here and there. But mostly I could wish that a half dozen of such intensely committed and capable Italian restaurateurs would open similar restaurants around the city.

GALILEO, 2014 P Street NW, Washington. Telephone: (202) 293-7191. Lunch: noon–2:30 pm Monday–Friday. Dinner: 5:30 pm–10 pm Monday–Thursday; 5:30 pm–10:30 pm Friday, Saturday. Closed Sunday. Cards: AE, DC, MC, V. Reservations required. Street parking. Full bar service.

Washington: Downtown
GARY'S
Steakhouse $$

Don't let the plush carpeting fool you into thinking that Gary's is anything other than a good steakhouse. The environment is dim, spacious and silken, but steak and roast beef are the heroes here, plus seafood pasta as a first course. Gary's is also known to grill very good fish, and the menu stretches to veal, rack of lamb or pork, and seafoods. Watch out for the overfancy. Sauces are not a strong point. Steaks are thick, well marbled and crusty. Don't tamper with success—enjoy large portions of good, simple food, a kind of Palm in a velvet cocoon.

GARY'S, 1800 M Street NW, Washington. Telephone: (202) 463-6470. Hours: 11:30 am–10 pm Monday–Friday; 6:30 pm–10:30 pm Saturday. Closed Sunday. Cards: AE, CB, DC, MC, V. Reservations required for lunch, suggested for dinner. Free parking in garage after 5 pm. Full bar service. Wheelchair access.

GEORGETOWN BAR & GRILL
American $$

The new Georgetown Bar & Grill has done a remarkable job of looking as if it has been there forever. The ceiling is crisscrossed with dark wood beams that seem to glow from decades of polishing. The wooden floor looks burnished by wear and care. The tables and banquettes, the low dividers of curved wood and of green-tinged marble seem the work of tradition, not decoration. And the large circular bar recalls a gathering place of generations. There are casual kinds of meals called barroom fare, and more serious (and more expensive) main courses called principal dishes: grilled duck with green peppercorns, sauteed veal, ginger crab cakes, fillet of beef with sun-dried tomato compote, stuffed pastas, spareribs and parchment-baked fish. And there are combination plates of seafoods, fish or meat with pasta, and grilled shrimp which is cooked with no oil or salt. Of course there are plentiful appetizers and desserts, and a four-course champagne brunch on Sundays. This is the new American cooking, bearing an obvious family resemblance to 209½, Mrs. Simpson's and Foggy Bottom Cafe. The food is fresh, pretty, colorful and imaginative. Familiar dishes are prepared with a twist that enhances their character. The club sandwich is made with chicken breast grilled to order, the fried squid comes with fresh horseradish or a chunky and fresh-tasting raw tomato sauce, crab cakes with a superlative tartar sauce and a cocktail sauce much improved by fresh horseradish. Six belon oysters with an aromatic pink sauce of shallots and raspberry vinegar is not only delightful, it is a bargain. The best of the Georgetown Bar & Grill are the old standards, here raised above the ordinary: a fine fat hamburger, those excellent calamari and belon oysters, crab cakes crisped and whipped to unusual lightness, a solid and zesty chili, and enormous hot sandwiches layered with varied textures and flavors.

GEORGETOWN BAR AND GRILL, 1310 Wisconsin Avenue NW, Washington. Telephone: (202) 337-7777. Breakfast: 7:30 am–10:30 am daily. Lunch: 11:30 am–2:30 pm daily. Dinner: 5:30 pm–midnight Tuesday–Saturday; 5:30 pm–11 pm Sunday, Monday. Cards: AE, CB, DC, MC, V. Reservations suggested. Valet parking. Full bar service.Wheelchair access.

appetizers and soups

minestrone with fontina cheese   3.75
cold fresh belon oysters with raspberry-shallot sauce   5.95
salad of romaine and watercress with choice of dressings   3.75
fried calamari with horseradish or raw tomato sauce   3.95
lightly creamed shrimp chowder   4.50
honey-barbecued sparerib appetizer (4)   4.75
miniature crab cakes with horseradish sauce   5.95
white bean chili bowl with chopped onions and peppers   3.75

seafood appetizers for two: two belon oysters, four miniature crabcakes
and fried calamari with seafood sauces   9.95

*

bar room fare

hamburger with thick-cut bacon and roquefort cheese   6.95
broiled scrod with lemon and fresh herbs   7.95
chicken caesar salad foggy bottom café   7.95
fresh chicken club sandwich   6.95
calf's liver with crisp bacon and onion marmalade   7.95
cold shrimp with red caviar, served over linguini salad   8.95
shrimp or chicken salad louis   8.95

*

principal dishes

duck grilled with green peppercorns   12.95
sauté of veal with belgian endive and cream   13.95
ginger crab cakes with seafood sauces   15.95
jumbo grilled shell steak with béarnaise sauce   14.95
center cut fillet steak served with sun-dried tomato compote   16.95
parchment baked fresh fish with leeks and carrots, hollandaise sauce
honey-barbecued spareribs with crisp potatoes   half rack   7.95
pasta of the day

Washington: Georgetown
GEPPETTO
Italian $

Geppetto is as cute as ever, set with cuckoo clocks and puppets, and as nice as ever, its young servers majoring in graciousness. Geppetto is as slow as ever, its staff overburdened by its popularity. And the food is as mixed as ever. The pizza is terrific, the yeasty crust either thick or thin, as you choose, highly peppered and spread with chunks of tomato and a sea of cheese. Toppings are overpriced, so the best order is a plain thick-crusted Sicilian pizza. Also try the sandwich of deep-fried eggplant, prosciutto and ricotta, and the dessert of creamy, chocolate-studded ricotta pie. Within Geppetto's short menu—sandwiches, salads, pizzas and a few daily specials—there is enough to please.

GEPPETTO, 2917 M Street NW, Washington. Telephone: (202) 333-2602. Hours: noon–11:30 pm Monday–Thursday; noon–1:30 am Friday, Saturday; 4 pm–11:30 pm Sunday. Cards: AE, CB, DC, MC, V. No reservations. Street parking. Full bar service. Wheelchair access.

Washington: Georgetown
GERMAINE'S ✻
Vietnamese $$

Germaine's is an Asian restaurant: Vietnamese, Thai, Korean, Chinese. But more than that, it is Germaine Swanson's restaurant: an outlet for her culinary invention in her Asian culinary tradition. Thus, the dishes to watch most closely are the daily specials, Germaine's newest. There is too much to choose from for a single dinner, from regal-looking whole fish and pork cooked with eggplant to chicken with basil or lemon sauce or governor's style. One of the favorites, and rightly so, is pine cone fish, a large, very fresh fillet deeply scored so it curls in the frying to resemble a giant pine cone. The surfaces are crisp and greaseless, the interior is white and steamy, and there is a soy sauce dip to moisten it. This is a dish that grows on you. The secret of Germaine's food is quality and freshness in the ingredients, delicacy in the seasonings—with no MSG. So stir-fried dishes are bright and crunchy, charcoal-grilled sates are juicy and fragrant and tender. Of course there are slips. The shrimp cakes as appetizers have been heavy, and paper-fried shrimp—pretty little deep-fried triangles of shrimp paste in rice paper—have been marred by greasiness. But in general this is light and fresh food, none more so than asparagus marinated in a soy-ginger sauce and topped by shredded chicken breast or an extraordinary scallop salad. The freshness is complemented by handsome pottery vases and flowers on the tables, by smoothly formal waiters and by the skylit dining room decorated with stunning photographs of Asia. The trick at Germaine's is to order the restaurant's special dishes, not to fall back on familiar Chinese offerings. And take along your fish-loving friends to share what are probably the best dishes in the house.

GERMAINE'S, 2400 Wisconsin Avenue NW, Washington. Telephone: (202) 965-1185. Lunch: noon–2:30 pm Monday–Friday. Dinner: 6 pm–10 pm Sunday–Thursday, 6 pm–11 pm Friday, Saturday. Cards: AE, CB, DC, MC, V. Reservations suggested. Street parking or nearby lot. Full bar service.

Here is a modern pub, with wood tables, hanging lamps and tableware far more stylish than a hotel location would suggest. The large room is subdivided, with much of the seating in booths—clean-cut and cozy, with plenty of space for an active bar crowd and quiet dinner. Even the drinks are out of the ordinary; a tiny bottle of Tabasco is served with the bloody mary, and a lightly alcoholic "fluff" is offered as an alternative to a full drink. The choice of house wines is worthwhile, the beer selection extensive. The menu lends itself to nibbling, with appetizers such as nachos, hummus, a lumpfish caviar platter and crisped potato skins. Most of the food is a cut above standard singles-bar fare. Inventive soups, sandwiches (roast beef with brie and watercress) and salads (smoked turkey with lingonberries and wild rice, a high-quality chicken salad that could have used less sesame oil, and chopped liver). There are tempura, veal with mushrooms and madeira, and crab meat ravioli, plus a good fresh fish special, a strip steak of decent quality and fettuccine primavera. The smoked salmon and onion omelet is soft and moist. Most important, there are hamburgers, excellent ones. So there are plains and fancies on this menu, and some of the plain things are done unusually well: oysters with a hail of fresh horseradish plus original and fresh-tasting chunky tomato sauce; french fries that are thin and

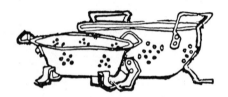

crunchy. As for desserts, they are as rich and gooey as American tradition demands—including "serious milk-shakes" and a multichocolate bombe called "chocolatus maximus."

G. PINCHOT'S, 1615 Rhode Island Avenue, Washington. Telephone: (202) 293-6811. Lunch: 11:30 am–2:30 pm daily. Dinner: 5:30 pm–10 pm daily. Cards: AE, CB, DC, MC, V. Reservations suggested. Free valet parking for dinner only. Full bar service.

Washington: Downtown
HARVEY'S
Seafood $$$

If you know your way around Harvey's, it is a fine seafood restaurant. But it is full of pitfalls. Its main assets are impeccable ingredients, from the crab meat and flounder to the California wines and top-brand liquors. Tables are well spaced, roomy, but the lighting makes reading the menu an effort. No matter, the waiters and waitresses offer real assistance in ordering, and cheerfully pace your meal as you wish, for speed or dallying. Soups are thick and creamy, dull or conservative, depending on your point of view. Plainest dishes are best: crab imperial with giant soft lumps of backfin and just a light wash of sauce, tiny and perfectly sauteed softshells in season (with superfluous grapes), plain grilled fish that could not be better. Vegetables are inventive, coleslaw well made. But steer clear of French elaborations and stick to plain local seafood.

HARVEY'S, 1001 18th Street NW, Washington. Tele-phone: (202) 833-1858. Hours: 11 am–10:30 pm Monday–Friday; 5 pm–10:30 pm Saturday, Sunday. Closed Sunday during summer. Cards: AE, CB, DC, MC, V. Reservations suggested. Free valet parking for dinner. Full bar service. Wheelchair access at K Street entrance.

HELEN'S ✳
American   **$$**

Here's new American cuisine to the utmost with an
oriental accent and trendy touches from around the
world. In a fresh, pretty second-floor dining room
caterer Helen Wasserman has made a successful transi-
tion to a hard-striving restaurant likely on its way to
excellence. Many appetizers are worth the wait, most
notably the pepper-spiked, cheese-filled won tons,
spring rolls filled with chicken and black mushrooms,
and the bright-colored vegetable terrine. Among main
dishes, seafood and oriental offerings seemed most
reliable, and the accompanying vegetables are often
excellent. Try shrimp with cabbage and caviar, a startling
combination that works.

HELEN'S, 1805 18th Street NW, Washington. Tele-
phone: (202) 483-4444. Dinner: 6 pm–11 pm Monday–
Thursday; 6 pm–1 am Friday, Saturday; 5:30 pm–9:30
pm Sunday. Cards: MC, V. Reservations suggested.
Street parking or nearby lot. Full bar service.

Appetizers:

Soup du Jour	2.25
Herbed Chicken Pate/Fresh Tomato Sauce	4.25
Spring Roll / Nuoc Mam Sauce	3.50
Cheese Filled Wontons with Guacamole	3.25
Smoked Salmon and Avocado Terrine, Basil Vinaigrette	4.95
Oriental Duck Salad, Roasted Duck with	
Julienne of Vegetables	5.95
Helen's Salad, Boston Lettuce, Bacon Lardons,	
Wonton Curls, Julienne of Vegetables, Cashews	2.95
Scallop and Shrimp Salad on Avocado Half	5.25
Cheese Fondue For Two	3.50

Entrees:

Breast of Chicken with Tarragon in Mustard Sauce	9.95
Veal Scallops with Shitake Mushrooms and Cream	14.50
Filet of Lamb with Fresh Herbs	17.95
Calves Liver with Marsala and Sage	11.95
Scallops with Julienne of Grape Fruit	
with ginger and chives	13.75
Oriental Baby Quail/Soy Dipping Sauce	13.50
Stir Fry Szechuan Shrimp with	
Red and Green Peppers	13.95
Stir Fry Chicken - Inquire	9.95
Fettucine with Sweet Red Pepper Sauce	
and Julienne of Zucchini	9.25
Seafood Selection - Inquire	—
Vegetable Curry with Chutney, Steamed Rice	9.25

HOUSE OF HUNAN
Chinese $$

Consider all previous reviews of House of Hunan super-ceded. This once-wonderful Chinese restaurant is resting on its laurels just when the downtown Chinese competition has heated up. The change is immediately apparent in the dining rooms, where tables are wedged so tight that one diner may have to get up so that those at another table can leave. The formerly exquisite, crispy shrimp balls are still light inside, but grease laden outside, and the spring rolls are both greasy and filled with little but soggy cabbage. Bon bon chicken is no more piquant or exciting than a peanut butter sandwich, and the once delectable minced squab soup, no longer served in a charming bamboo cup, lacks the rich flavor of former days. For main courses, you can get very good Peking duck, but it ought to be displayed and carved tableside rather than brought after being carved in the kitchen—with not a lot of meat to show for it. And otherwise the food is merely ordinary, the crispy prawns tasting as if they had sat too long for the batter to stay crisp, the Neptune's catch good enough seafoods but in a sluggish and nondescript sauce, not to mention an underfried potato basket. Lamb is shaved thin and has lost taste as well as bite. In short, nothing but the prices are now above run-of-the-mill. The House of Hunan once showed us what a Chinese restaurant could be, in terms of beautiful and serene surroundings, outstandingly thoughtful service and food that was full of surprises, all good ones. It could now match with any pedestrian shopping-center Chinese restaurant and be distinguished only by its high prices.

HOUSE OF HUNAN, 1900 K Street NW, Washington. Telephone: (202) 293-9111. Lunch: 11:30 am–3 pm Monday–Saturday; 12:30 pm–3 pm Sunday. Dinner: 5 pm–10:15 daily. Cards: AE, CB, DC, MC, V. Reservations suggested. Street parking or nearby garages. Full bar service. Wheelchair access.

CHEF'S SUGGESTIONS

左 公 雞
* General Tso's Chicken   11.95
HOT! Chunks of boneless chicken sauteed with Chef's special sauce

湘 江 鴨 塊
Duck with Young Ginger Roots   13.95
Pieces of boneless duck sauteed with green pepper and young ginger roots

核 桃 脆 皮 蝦
* Crispy Prawns with Walnuts   13.95
HOT! Sliced prawns with walnuts cooked in tangy sauce

湖 南 脆 皮 魚
* Crispy Whole Fish Hunan Style   16.95
HOT! Sea bass deep-fried until crisp coated with sweet and spicy sauce

龍 蝦 鬆
Sauteed Lobster Soong   18.95
Ground lobster prepared in Chef's secret sauce then wrapped in lettuce

陳 皮 牛
* Orange Beef   13.95
HOT! Tender chunks of top-choice steak sauteed with orange-flavored sauce— House of Hunan's original creation— recipe used nowhere else in DC

湘 綺 蝦 片
Lake Tung Ting Shrimp   13.95
Shrimp marinated with broccoli, straw mushrooms and egg whites in a white sauce

海 鮮 雀 巢
Neptune's Catch in Bird's Nest   16.95
Sauteed crabmeat, prawns, scallops and sliced fish served in a delicious nest made from crisp potatoes

葡 萄 魚
Crispy Whole Fish in Grape Wine Sauce   16.95
Boneless sea bass deep-fried until crispy, sauteed with Chef's special grape wine sauce

北 京 鴨
Peking Duck   22.95
A young seasoned duckling slowly grilled over an open fire until the skin is crisp and golden—first the delicate skin is sliced then the meat is carved separately—served with homemade crepes, scallions and Hoisin sauce

When you open a flashy big-city pub these days, you gotta serve good stuff. Just look at Houston's. The old-brick arches and jungle of greenery, the silk-shaded little brass lamps over the oiled wood booths, the gleaming brass and the filigree of wrought iron. We down our hamburgers in California lushness these days. Those burgers are thick patties of ground-in-the-house chuck grilled over hickory and oak. And the french fries are far from the old crinkle cuts. These are long, dark crusty ones cut from potatoes that are not only fresh, but of the proper mealy and faintly sweet variety, cooked in good oil and at the right temperature. Remember when coleslaw was bought in tubs with a month of shelf life? Well, it still is, but not at Houston's, where the slaw tastes made that day, coarsely chopped and lightly creamy. Good slaw, and not oversweetened. Unfortunately nearly everything else at Houston's is oversweetened: the salad dressings, the cinnamon apples, the baked beans, even the chili. In all, Houston's is a pub as friendly as you'd expect a Texan to be, and as efficient as the best of America's chain restaurants. Its food is no major addition to Washington's larder, but it is good enough to show that pub food has come a long way.

HOUSTON'S, 1065 Wisconsin Avenue NW, Washington. Telephone: (202) 338-7760. Hours: 11:30 am–midnight Sunday–Thursday; 11:30 am–1 pm Friday, Saturday. Cards: AE, MC, V. No reservations. Street parking. Full bar service. Wheelchair access.

HUNAN DYNASTY
Chinese   **$**

The Hunan Dynasty is an example of what makes
Chinese restaurants such reliable choices. A great
restaurant? It is not. A good value? Definitely. A
restaurant to fit nearly any diner's need? Probably.
First, it is attractive. Second, service is a strong priority.
Third, the food is largely good if not quite wonderful,
and it is proudly arranged on platters and garnished
with vegetables carved into flowers. This is the kind of
Chinese restaurant sophisticated enough to have a
separate wine list and to stock good Asian beers. Then
there is the menu, long and eclectic, with samplings
from Szechuan, Peking, Canton and Hunan styles.
Prices are moderate, and you get a lot for your money.
The best of the appetizers is sweet-and-sour spareribs,
small juicy pieces that are rich with the flavor of five-
spice powder and sweetened soy marinade. As for main
dishes, don't take the "hot and spicy" asterisks too
seriously. Hunan Dynasty is a top-flight neighborhood
restaurant—with good food, caring service and very fair
prices—that is attractive enough to set a mood for
celebration and easygoing enough for an uncomplicated
dinner with the family after work.

HUNAN DYNASTY, 215 Pennsylvania Avenue SE,
Washington. Telephone: (202) 546-6161. Hours: 11
am–10 pm Monday–Friday; 11:30 am–10 pm Saturday,
Sunday. Cards: AE, CB, DC, MC, V. Reservations
suggested. Street parking. Full bar service.

Washington: Downtown
IRON GATE INN
Middle Eastern $$

When warm weather comes, it would not matter if the Iron Gate Inn charged you for bringing your lunch; its garden is so delightful that people would eat there no matter what. The old inn is charming in the winter, too, but summer is its season. The food is Middle Eastern, nothing you would cross a desert for, but perfectly acceptable cooking at moderate prices. The hummos and baba ghanouj are served with warmed pita. The baked eggplant with lamb and rice absorbs the flavors of tomato, olive oil and onions to turn into a succulent near-paste. Stuffed grape leaves, stuffed cabbage and kibbe have all improved in recent years, but not the kebabs. The baklava is very light and sweetened with restraint, an outstanding version of this syrupy confection. The fare is all at least average, and enhanced by being served in a grape arbor, to the sound of birds rather than manmade music.

IRON GATE INN, 1734 N Street NW, Washington. Telephone: (202) 737-1370. Hours: 11:30 am–10:30 pm daily. Cards: AE, DC, MC, V. No reservations for lunch, suggested for dinner. Street parking or garage a half block away. Full bar service. Wheelchair access.

MIDDLE EAST CHICKEN 7.95
Roasted with sauteed tomatoes, onions & rice.

BREAST OF CHICKEN SUMAC............................... 7.95
Served with rice.

ROCK CORNISH HEN KABAB 8.50
Broiled Tomatoes, Onions and Peppers. Served with Rice.

SHEESH KABAB 11.95
Broiled Lamb, with Tomatoes, Onions and Rice.

BEEF SHEESH KABAB 11.95
Broiled Filet Mignon Cubes - Tomatoes, Onions and Rice.

SHRIMP KABAB.. 12.50
Broiled Jumbo Shrimp with Tomatoes, Onions & Rice.

LAMB CURRY 8.95
Specially Prepared from Our Own Recipes. Served with Mango Chutney.

SHRIMP CURRY 9.25
Specially Prepared from Our Own Recipes. Served with Mango Chutney.

VEGETARIAN CURRY 8.25
Made from Fresh Fruit and Vegetables. Served with Mango Chutney.

WARAQ INAB MAHSI 7.95
Grape Leaves Stuffed with Ground Lamb and Rice.

MALFUF MAHSI 7.50
Cabbage Stuffed with Ground Lamb and Rice.

KUSA 7.75
Squash Stuffed with Ground Lamb and Rice.

MNAZZALEH.. 8.50
Baked Eggplant Stuffed with Ground Lamb, Toasted Pine Nuts and
Baked in Tomato Sauce and Rice.

KIFTA... 8.95
Lamb Meatballs Cooked in Tomato Sauce and Rice.

KIBBEH 8.95
Baked Ground Lamb, Cracked Wheat and Toasted Pine Nuts.
Served with Grape Leaves.

MAUZAT KHROUF 9.25
Specially Prepared Lamb Shank in a Wine and Tomato Sauce over Rice.

ROAST LEG OF LAMB 8.75
With Pine Nuts and Lamb Rice.

MAFTOOL - (Middle Eastern Cous Cous) 8.50
Prepared with Craked Wheat and Chunks of Tender Lamb and
vegetables, in a light sauce.

MIDDLE EAST GARDEN SALAD 7.50
Feta Cheese Ham, Breast of Chicken, Greek Olives and Pickled Turnips.
                              Blue Cheese Dressing .... .75

Washington: Downtown
JEAN LOUIS ✳
French $$$

Washington's best restaurants nowadays would be any
city's best, and if Jean Louis were in Paris, New York or
Tokyo its star would shine no less brightly. Downstairs
in the Watergate, this small restaurant has walls paved
with cloth in various shades of orange and mirrors that
subtly enlarge the space. As good as it always has been,
much has improved. The service is conducted by an
outstanding team; the wine list has been revamped to an
exceptional array—with acceptable prices. And Jean
Louis' cooking is ever more imaginative and sure. The
touches of surprise—tomato slices in the crab cake,
ginger with the salmon mille feuille, rosettes of mozzarella
with the shrimp and hearts of palm salad, duck with
dates, honey and cumin—are dealt with a light hand.
This is subtle food, and beautiful, with color and texture
as carefully orchestrated as is flavor. It is also presented
in a menu designed to ease your choices: Pick the
number of courses (two, three or four plus dessert), then
the dishes within those courses. You can even opt for
appropriate wines by the glass to accompany each
course. The best of Jean Louis hearkens to his roots in
southwest France: He does wonders with truffles (as
breading for sweetbreads or sauce for crayfish) and with
foie gras (sauteed with pears or peaches, studding a
mushroom or leek terrine). Whatever he does with
rabbit is likely to be exquisite. On the other hand, his
crab cakes don't satisfy a Maryland sensibility, and
desserts are undergoing renovation. Jean Louis remains
as interesting as it is excellent.

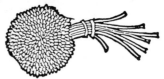

JEAN LOUIS, 2650 Virginia Avenue NW (in the Watergate Hotel), Washington. Telephone: (202) 298-4488. Lunch: noon–2 pm Monday–Friday. Dinner: 6:30 pm–10 pm Monday–Saturday. Closed Sunday and month of August. Cards: AE, CB, DC, MC, V. Reservations required. Free valet parking. Full bar service. Wheelchair access.

Washington: Downtown
JEAN-PIERRE
French   **$$$**

New cuisine, old cuisine, the lines were drawn by the French restaurants of the world in the last decade, and now, thank goodness, they have been allowed to blur. Thus, a restaurant like Jean-Pierre serves some new, some old, and, most important, all a reflection of its chef's considerable talent. Consider the cold appetizers: While innumerable restaurants are serving paper-thin slices of home-cured salmon, chef Gerard Vettraino serves his supple raw salmon on a cloud of highly seasoned whipped cream, and surrounds it with morsels of multihued marinated vegetable salads. Fish pates are difficult tasks, and even here they can be heavy or dull; but they can also be a velvety salmon rillettes or an intriguing concoction of chopped oysters. Main dishes are more traditional: a beautifully roasted chicken with tarragon, a rockfish fillet grilled to smokiness and topped with a froth of buttery mustard sauce, perhaps rare slices of roasted lamb or pale and moist medallions of veal with tiny wedges of lemon. Duck is a favorite here, rolled up on a trolley and carved tableside. What are untraditional are the garnishes of miniature bundles of crisply cooked vegetables, a nicety that raises very good food to grandeur. Jean-Pierre also accompanies dinner with what might be the best potatoes au gratin in town. Not only is the food very good in this small and quiet restaurant, but the service also shows its many years of experience, and the dining room has been redone into a contemporary jewel. Jean-Pierre's wine list shows meticulous concern for the quality of the food and for a varied range of budgets. And among the desserts—in general good if not outstanding—is a truly luscious omelet souffle, at its best when filled with fresh raspberries. In all, Jean-Pierre has matured into a very satisfying French restaurant.

JEAN-PIERRE, 1835 K Street NW, Washington. Telephone: (202) 466-2022. Lunch: noon–2 pm Monday–Friday. Dinner: 6 pm–10 pm Monday–Friday; 6 pm–10:30 pm Saturday. Closed Sunday. Cards: AE, CB, DC, MC, V. Reservations required. Full bar service. Valet parking. Jacket and tie required.

Washington: Downtown
J. J. MELLON'S
American $$

Washington's old downtown is springing to life, with new hotels, the refurbished National Theatre and the lusciously restored Old Post Office. So, while you can eat well from the Pavillion's food stands and adequately in the several full-service restaurants, for more quiet and comfort—and probably better food—J. J. Mellon's is worth knowing. The best of J. J. Mellon's is not the limited dinner menu, but the post-theater suppers and desserts. For heavy fare, the steaks and simple seafoods will do, but after the show, an appetizer and dessert shows this kitchen at its best.

J. J. MELLON'S, 1201 Pennsylvania Avenue NW, Washington. Telephone: (202) 737-5700. Hours: 11:30 am–10 pm Monday–Friday. Closed Saturday, Sunday. Cards: AE, CB, DC, MC, V. No reservations. Garage parking. Full bar service. Wheelchair access.

Restaurant fashions, like others, wax and wane; and for some years the Jockey Club has been waxing after being dubbed a Reaganite hangout. What it offers is a dining room arranged for a good deal of coziness, trimmed in dark wood and soft leather banquettes and spacious tables. The food is presented by a staff steeped in experience and schooled in cosseting the mighty. As for the food, it is high-quality standard fare in the French mode with American accents. Few show-stoppers, but heart-stopping prices. What the kitchen does best is crab, and the crab cakes are as good as crab cakes get. Large, sweet, snowy lumps of crab, perfectly seasoned and lightly bound, rolled in fresh crumbs and sauteed in butter. Outstanding, but they should be at the price. And they keep company with insipid and flavorless soup, soggy squab in a characterless sauce and a king's ransom of wild rice that somehow lacks savor. The pastry is oversweet, and souffles look pallid, though the menu includes an utterly delicious orange-sauced custard. Scallops are carefully cooked and pleasantly sauced with cream and tarragon, but nothing beyond crab or custard stands above the crowd. At such expense, one expects more flair. The wine list is more

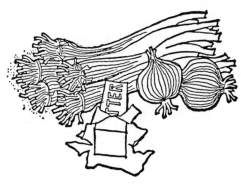

exciting than the menu, with special emphasis on the hard-to-find Californians. But like the food, its prices would dent a Reagan budget.

JOCKEY CLUB, 2100 Massachusetts Avenue NW, Washington. Telephone: (202) 293-2100. Breakfast: 6:30 am–11 am Monday–Sunday. Brunch: noon–2:30 pm Sunday. Lunch: noon–2:30 pm Monday–Saturday. Dinner: 6 pm–10:30 pm Monday–Sunday. Cards: AE, CB, DC, MC, V. Reservations suggested. Valet parking. Full bar service. Wheelchair access. Non-smoking area. Jacket and tie required.

Entrées

Crab Cakes Jockey Club 21.50
Scallops Sautées Orléannaise aux Petits Légumes 19.75
Escalopes de Saumon a la Vapeur,
Julienne de Légumes 22.00
Dover Sole Sauté Meunière 21.75
Crabmeat Sauté Dijonnaise 23.25

Poitrine de Canard Rotie aux Framboises et Poivre Vert 19.25
Supréme de Cornish Hen Grillée, Sauce a l'Estragon 18.00
Mignons de Veau aux Champignons 22.25
Tournedo Rossini 23.50
Rack of Lamb, Bouquetière (for two) 24.75 per person
Steak Diane Flambé 24.50
Calf's Liver Sauté aux Raisins 19.50

Paillard de Veau Grillé 21.50
Sirloin Steak Maître d'Hôtel 23.50
Chateaubriand (for two) 24.00 per person
Double Lamb Chops Vert Pré 22.50
Filet Mignon, Sauce Béarnaise 22.25

Washington: Downtown
JOE AND MO'S
Steakhouse

$$

Joe and Mo's has become a hit restaurant where being seen is as important as being fed. A meat-and-potatoes (or, these days, fish-and-salad) place, where lately most of the pizzazz has been in the dining room; the staff know how to make everybody feel like a presidential adviser. But the kitchen sometimes forgets how to make its potato pancakes crisp, its fish moist. Breadings and sauces are heavy. The bread, however, is outstanding. The best of Joe and Mo's may be its breakfast, when the clever menu is an eye-opener itself, and the surroundings add luxury to an otherwise mundane meal.

JOE AND MO'S, 1211 Connecticut Avenue NW, Washington. Telephone: (202) 659-1211. Hours: 11:30 am–10:45 pm Monday–Friday. Breakfast: 7:30 am–10 am Monday–Friday. Dinner: 6 pm–10:45 pm Saturday. Closed Sunday. Cards: AE, CB, DC, MC, V. Reservations suggested for dinner and required for lunch. Valet parking for dinner only. Full bar service. Wheelchair access. Non-smoking area.

KALORAMA CAFE
Natural Foods $

Like a '60s coffeehouse, Kalorama Cafe wears a home-spun lived-in and cared-for look. Assorted printed tablecloths, brick walls and an open kitchen make this tiny restaurant look neighborly, and the blackboard outside the door, listing the daily specials, acts as a welcome mat. The short menu is close to vegetarian, with only fish and shrimp breaking the vegetable barrier. Tempura—either fish, shrimp or plain vegetable—is available every day, and it is excellent, its batter light and wispy, the shrimp large and juicy, each vegetable fully cooked but still crisp. Broiled fish is fresh and soy seasoned, cooked beautifully. Accompanying salads are dressed with an interesting combination of soy and lemon. Even the rice on the plates, brown rice with soy sauce and scallions, is admirable. Daily specials are an eclectic mix of lasagne, Indonesian vegetables, lentil pates and the like. Two cautions are needed: This very casual, amateur operation can be unreliable, and desserts are heavy and wheaten, tasting like something you ought to eat rather than want to eat. Sometimes there is folk music in the evenings.

KALORAMA CAFE, 2228 18th Street NW, Washington. Telephone: (202) 667-1022. Brunch: 11 am–3 pm Sunday. Lunch: 11:30 am–3 pm Tuesday–Saturday. Dinner: 6 pm–10 pm Tuesday–Saturday. Closed Monday. No credit cards. Reservations suggested for large parties. Street parking or nearby lot. Beer and wine only. Wheelchair access.

Entreés . . .

All dinner specials are served with a salad

Vegetable Specials . . .

Vegetables Mornay steamed broccoli, carrots, zucchini, and mushrooms on a bed of brown rice with a wine and cheese sauce $6.95

Falafel, with bulghur served with tahini sauce $6.95

Broccoli-Tofu Stir-Fry w/brown rice, mushroom and ginger. $6.95

Tostada—w/w tortilla w/guac., let., tom., grate ched., & enchil. sauce. Served w/corn chips & salsa. $6.95

Nightly Vegetable Special

Seafood . . .

Fish and Chips fresh haddock, batter dipped and deep fried. $7.50

Broiled Fresh Haddock with tamari, garlic and served with brown rice. $7.50

Sauteed shrimp in Garlic served with brown rice. $8.50

Fish Mornay Broiled fish with a wine and cheese sauce and brown rice $7.50

Pasta . . .

Spinach Linguine prepared with herbs and garlic $6.50

Spinach Linguine prepared with tomato sauce and cheese $6.50

Spinach Linguine with clams and herbs and cream $7.50

Spinach Linguine with red clam sauce $7.50

Spiral w/w pasta with mushrooms, cream and parmesan $7.50

Homemade Carrot Pasta with broccoli, cream and parmesan. $7.50

Spiral w/w pasta with no dairy, broccoli and mushrooms and ginger sauce. $6.95

Tempura . . .

dipped in a whole wheat batter and deep fried

Shrimp and Vegetable Tempura $8.95

Fish and Vegetable Tempura $7.95

Vegetable and Tofu Tempura $7.95

Sandwiches . . .

Fresh Haddock Sandwich w/chips $4.50

Falafel a spicy mixture of chick peas deep fried served with lettuce, tomatoes, tahini dressing in pita bread $3.95

Cheese and Vegetable pita bread filled w/fresh vegetables & cheese, house dressing. $3.95

Open-Faced Cheese & Vegetable whole Wheat bread, vegetables and melted cheese. $4.50

Crabcake Sandwich with fries $4.95

Desserts . . .

Strawberry Shortcake our own short-cake with fresh strawberries and real cream. $2.25

Carob Honey Mousse $1.50

Banana Fritters batter fried bananas with whipped cream. $1.95

Honey Carrot Cake $1.75

Honey Cheesecake $1.95

Honey Cheesecake with strawberries. $2.50

KHYBER PASS
Afghan   **$**

Khyber Pass is a small, second-floor restaurant, with artifacts on the walls and a rock garden in the window. Service is solicitous and tends to be slow. The most memorable dish is aushak, homemade noodles filled with leeks or scallions and topped with yogurt, mint and a dab of tomato-meat sauce; the combination of flavors is luscious. A similar preparation also makes a soup, aush. The least-memorable dishes are those with spinach, which is cooked to a tasteless mush. Most of the main courses are kebabs, very aromatic from their marinades, tender and grill-crisped. The chicken is sometimes stringy, so lamb and beef may be better choices. The palow, a mound of rice and lamb seasoned with coriander and the sweet touch of caramelized carrot strips and raisins, is intriguing. Add a side dish of sauteed pumpkin or eggplant with yogurt and mint. The proper ending is a platter-size, paper-thin fried pastry dusted with cardamom, chopped pistachios and sugar, and cardamom tea. The bread is homemade but lacks flavor; though its texture is most enjoyable. Some dishes—the long-cooked spinach and cornstarch pudding—can be easily ignored, but the best offerings can be delectable.

KHYBER PASS, 2309 Calvert Street NW, Washington. Telephone: (202) 234-4632. Hours: Lunch: 11:30 am–2:30 pm Monday–Friday. Dinner: 5:30 pm–11 pm Monday–Sunday. No credit cards. Reservations accepted. Parking lot in rear. Full bar service.

ENTREES

QUABILI PALOW **7.50**
*Delicately seasoned pieces of lamb under a
mound of saffron rice, topped with carrot
strips and raisins. Served with small salad
and Afghan bread.*

SABSI CHALOW **7.65**
*Chunks of lamb in an onion and garlic - flavored
spinach sauce, served with white rice, small salad
and Afghan bread.*

KORMA CHALOW **7.95**
*Spicy beef stew served with rice, small salad
and Afghan bread.*

KABOB **10.50**
*Skewered chunks of lamb marinated in yogurt
and garlic, charcoal - broiled and served
with rice, small salad and Afghan bread.*

SHISH - LIK **9.95**
*Marinated chunks of beef, sauteed and
served with vegetable sauce, rice, small salad
and Afghan bread.*

KABOB - E - MURGH **9.50**
*Skewered chicken pieces marinated in yogurt and
spices, charcoal - broiled and served with rice,
small salad and Afghan bread.*

AUSHAK **7.25**
*Tiny leek - filled dumplings topped with yogurt
and meat sauce and sprinkled with mint, served
with small salad and Afghan bread.*

KHYBER PASS KABOB **10.50**
*Marinated chunks of lamb sauteed with onion
and tomatoes and topped with two eggs. Served
with vegetable sauce, rice, small salad and Afghan
bread.*

QEEMA KABOB **8.35**
*Ground beef prepared with onion, kale, eggs,
coriander spice and pepper. Grilled and served
with rice, small salad and Afghan bread.*

BAUNJAUN CHALOW **7.80**
*Sauteed eggplant cooked with a special sauce and
topped with yogurt. Served with rice, salad,
chunks of lamb and Afghan bread.*

BURAUNEE BAUNJAUN **6.95**
*Sauteed eggplant topped with yogurt and
meat sauce, served with small salad and
Afghan bread and side dish of rice.*

Washington: Capitol Hill
LA BRASSERIE ✳
French

$$

What a pleasure it has been to watch this little French restaurant grow better as well as larger. More charm is packed in the new dining rooms and the outdoor cafe than in the original two-story restaurant, and the service is attentive, even if close. The center of the menu is "cuisine gourmande," the daily inventions of the chef, which often include home-smoked salmon and seafood terrines, tranches of salmon herbed and perfectly grilled with a very light sauce. Look for asparagus in the lightest and crispest puff pastry, seafood bisque under a puff pastry lid and rare duck breast, which is particularly good. In general the food is beautifully prepared and painstakingly garnished with vegetable carvings and the like. Flaws? A lack of restraint, a too-active imagination, allowing excessively strong mustard sauce to swamp the lobster or too much sweetness to overwhelm a duck breast. Small flaws. If you like desserts rich and creamy, the creme brulee, white chocolate mousse or marquise au chocolat will compensate for any missteps.

LA BRASSERIE, 239 Massachusetts Avenue NE, Washington. Telephone: (202) 546-6066. Hours: 11:30 am–11:30 pm Monday–Saturday; 11:30 am–10 pm Sunday. Cards: AE, CB, MC, V. Reservations suggested. Street parking or valet parking. Full bar service. Non-smoking area.

Washington: Capitol Hill
LA COLLINE
French $$

At last Washington is developing a collection of middle-price restaurants with style and ambition, and La Colline is a good example. More handsome than one expects, on the ground floor of a large office building, the room has floral upholstery, high-back booths and a contemporary elegance. The menu is French and adventurous, seasonal and fresh, with good, fresh vegetables and excellent wines by the glass as well as by the bottle. There are flaws—soup of shallow flavor, seafood terrine that is oversalted and too gelatinous. But the platters, particularly the daily specials, hold to high standards, whether the season's first softshell crabs or thick, English-cut lamb chops with green peppercorn butter. The pastry chef also demonstrates skill; don't miss the Bavarian creams.

LA COLLINE, 400 North Capitol Street NW, Washington. Telephone: (202) 737-0400. Breakfast: 7 am–10 am Monday–Friday. Lunch: 11:30 am–3 pm Monday–Friday. Dinner: 6 pm–10 pm Monday–Saturday; 5 pm–9 pm Sunday. Cards: AE, CB, DC, MC, V. Reservations suggested. Street parking or garage parking after 5 pm. Full bar service. Wheelchair access.

For Washington, Lafitte is a change of taste. This is gutsy Creole cooking, with seasonings that draw your attention and stay in your memory. The shrimp and crayfish have been impeccable, far superior to those generally found in Washington restaurants. The barbecued shrimp are fat, juicy and fresh, blazed with cayenne, cloves and herbs. The crayfish bisque may look a benign pink and lull you with its fragrant creaminess, but it sears your tongue as it goes down. And the Cajun popcorn-batter fried crayfish tails are lovely little morsels. On the milder side, shrimp and crayfish etouffee are sturdily garlicked and sauced with fresh tomato puree. Duck Dumaine has a deep, mellow flavor in its mustard grown sauce, while more delicate dishes include baby coho salmon en croute. Rare in Washington is such an interesting choice of a la carte vegetables: There are pureed turnips and fried eggplant in addition to the usual creamed spinach, and there are pommes souffles, the little puffed potato slices so thin that they are all crust when they expand in the hot oil. In New Orleans the term lagniappe means a special little bonus. And at Lafitte it means hot muffins—jalapeño cornbread muffins if you are lucky—served as you sit down at lunch, or perhaps the crusty fried okra at dinner. It means a loaf of light french bread wrapped in a napkin and brought to the table as your main dish arrives; it means a pianist playing at lunch as well as dinner. Investigate the pastry cart, where there is pecan cheesecake and a fruit tart, or the kitchen's own ice creams and sherbets. But above all reserve a piece of the chocolate raspberry torte, which is dense, buttery, fudgy and intensely rich. All this and a lovely dining room, too, with Art Deco details, flourishes in wood, and mirrors on the walls and ceiling. The tables hold not only pretty sprays of exotic flowers, but also that most New Orleans of decorations—a bottle of Tabasco on each table.

LAFITTE, 1310 New Hampshire Avenue NW, Washington. Telephone: (202) 466-7978. Breakfast: 7 am–10:30 am Monday–Friday; 8 am–10:30 am Saturday, Sunday. Brunch: 11 am–2:30 pm Sunday. Lunch: 11:30 am–2:30 pm Monday–Friday. Dinner: 5:30 pm–10:30 pm Monday–Thursday; 6 pm–11 pm Friday, Saturday. Cards: AE, CB, DC, MC, V. Reservations suggested. Street parking or nearby lot. Full bar service. Jacket and tie required.

◆◆◆◆◆◆◆◆◆◆◆◆◆◆◆◆◆◆◆◆

Entrees

Trout Lafitte	
With roasted pecans and creole meuniere sauce	*11.50*
Crabmeat Imperial en Croute	*13.50*
Shrimp Étouffée	*13.50*
Louisiana Barbecued Shrimp	
Sautéed with fresh rosemary, cracked black pepper, garlic and a dash of Dixie beer	*14.75*
Cajun Prime Rib	
Served with New Orleans Bordelaise sauce	*17.50*
Chicken Boursin	
Stuffed with herbed cheese, sautéed and served with beurre blanc and chives	*9.50*
Canard Dumaine	
Braised in its own juices and served with sautéed potatoes and creole mustard	*12.75*
Pork Confit	
Braised in its own juices. Served with a piquante mustard sauce	*8.75*
Veal Esplanade	
Sautéed with plum tomatoes and bell peppers in a light white wine sauce	*13.50*
Filet Mignon—with Maitre d'Hotel Butter	*14.75*

Please ask your server for our fine selection of homemade desserts.

Washington: Downtown
LA FONDA
Mexican $

This gran dama of Mexican restaurants was here long before tacos were available in every supermarket and along every highway, but maturity is not its only claim for attention. Another is its sidewalk cafe, which is one of the less frenetic ones in Washington. The dining room, on the other hand, is an eccentric tiled space that is disconcertingly bright. While the menu is predictable and the cooking unexceptional, La Fonda has certain culinary charm in its mix-and-match choices. The wisest selection is a tray with assorted tidbits such as shredded beef and chicken, a small pottery bowl of very good refried beans, mounds of cheese, shredded lettuce and chopped tomato, onions and hot peppers, and sour cream sauce, with tortillas fried in various forms. All you need are a lazy afternoon, a couple bottles of Dos Equis beer and a tray of such nibblings to layer upon one another.

LA FONDA, 1639 R Street NW, Washington. Telephone: (202) 232-6965. Brunch: noon–3 pm Sunday. Lunch: 11:30 am–3 pm Monday–Friday. Dinner: 5 pm–11 pm Monday–Saturday. Cards: AE, CB, DC, MC, V. Reservations accepted for parties of five or more. Street parking. Full bar service. Non-smoking area.

CARNES Y AVES

Pinchos Aztecos 8.95
Tender Marinated Skewered Beef,
Charcoal Broiled and served with
Mexican Rice

Poc Chuc Yucateca 9.50
A Native Mayan Dish of Sliced
Marinated Pork served with
Black Beans and Roasted
Red Onions

Pollo en Mole 8.25
From the Puebla Region — their
famous Salsa de Mole with a
touch of Chocolate. Served over
Tender Poached Chicken

Pollito Pibil 8.95
A Whole Baby Hen marinated in
Fine Herbs, Mayan Spices, Wrapped
in a Banana Leaf and Baked Slowly
*A Dish from the
Yucatan Region of Mexico*

Bistec Tampiqueno 10.50
Charcoal Grilled Steak served
with an Enchilada, Quesadilla,
Black Beans and Guacamole

**Carne Asada
a La Mexicana 9.25**
Charcoal Broiled Tender Steak,
marinated with a blend of Mexican
Spices and served with Rice and
Fresh Guacamole Salad

Arroz Con Pollo 7.25
Fluffy Mexican Rice, Sauteed
Chicken, Peppers and Tomatoes
simmered with Chorizo Sausage
and Ham (Allow 25 minutes
for preparation)

Relleno de Cerdo 8.75
Rolled Tender Pork baked slowly
with native spices. Served
with an almond sauce.

Carne de Torito Chihuahuense 11.95
La Fonda's Choicest Strip Steak as prepared
in the Cattle Region of Mexico, garnished
with Sauteed Fresh Vegetables
*Ask your waiter for the Spicy
Marinade if desired.*

PESCADOS Y MARISCOS

Pescado Celestun 9.50
Fish Filet, gently poached then
baked with Achiote and Native
Mayan Spices, served with
Fresh Vegetables

Camarones al Mezcal 10.95
Tender Gulf Shrimp enhanced with
Mezcal and baked in a Flavorful
Cream Sauce

Nopalitos Navegantes 9.75
Gulf Shrimp and Baby Mexican
Cactus lightly sauteed and served
over a Bed of Rice

Pescado a la Veracruzana 9.95
Fish Veracruz style
sauteed with fresh peppers,
onions and ripe fresh tomatoes

(25 minutes for preparation on all seafood dishes)

Washington: Downtown
LA MAREE
French   **$$**

A small restaurant in the traditional style. La Maree has
retained a following for years as a reasonably reliable
French restaurant that concentrates largely on seafood.
But this is no plain fish house: Its seafood is simmered
in soups, baked in terrines, sauced grandly. And the
prices reflect the complexity. La Maree is one of the
city's lesser lights among the small French restaurants
downtown, but one that often enough shines brightly.

LA MAREE, 1919 I Street, Washington. Telephone:
(202) 659-4447. Lunch: 11:30 am–2:30 pm Monday–
Friday. Dinner: 5:30 pm–10:30 pm Monday–Friday;
5:30 pm–1:30 am Saturday. Closed Sunday. Cards: AE,
CB, DC, MC, V. Reservations suggested. Parking lot.
Full bar service.

Washington: Downtown
LA PLAZA
Latin American   **$$**

La Plaza's menu makes clear the distinction between
Mexican and Spanish food, and adds charcoal-broiled
steaks and fish to the mix. What's more, it serves them
all in a sophisticated uptown dining room that reminds
one how charming Adams-Morgan style can be. Prices
are reasonable, even more so when the quality and
quantity of food is taken into consideration. But the
cooking style is rustic and homey rather than refined.
Look for lots of celery and onion crunch and acid zest to
the ceviche, for instance. Duck is orange flavored, as one
expects in France, but this Spanish version has a lighter
and less sweet sauce, and the meat is juicy, the skin

crisp. Fish is fresh, prepared simply. In all, this is a good neighborhood restaurant with more ambition and flair than most.

LA PLAZA, 1847 Columbia Road NW, Washington. Telephone: (202) 667-1900. Hours: noon–midnight daily. Cards: AE, CB, DC, MC, V. Reservations suggested. Valet parking. Full bar service. Wheelchair access.

Washington: Downtown
LAURIOL PLAZA ✱
Latin American

$$

The first page of the menu lists appetizers and light entrees, but many of the appetizers are larger than light entrees. Quesadillas, for instance, are crisped flour tortillas sandwiched with melted cheese, onions and green chilies, topped with a taco cup filled with guacamole. Oozing cheese, greasy and spicy, each is as large and as filling as a pizza, easily a meal or the kind of late-night snack that holds you until lunch the next day. The mussels are excellent, seasoned with garlic, fresh ginger and sherry. There are, of course, nachos, a whole order or half, plus a ceviche that is not the best in town but pleasantly tart and mildly peppered, its chunks of thick white fish a little spongy but reasonably fresh. You can also get something so simple as avocados or fried bananas to start. Or quiche, a remnant from the pre-Latin days; even omelets or a chef's salad. Among main dishes there are four categories: Spanish, Mexican, charcoal-broiled and the daily specials, offerings like trout stuffed with crab meat or marinated lamb chops. The cooking outstrips all but a few of the dozens of Mexican restaurants from one end of the beltway to the other. Which doesn't mean you should overlook the Spanish food. The zarzuela de mariscos, though an alarming turmeric yellow, which with its red pimientos looks like a Day-Glo still life, is a mountain of carefully cooked seafood. And the best steak buy in town might be Lauriol Plaza's bistec a la criolla. In other words, Lauriol Plaza cuts a wide swath, from snacks to grand dinners, in a Manhattanesque dining room with an ethnic mood.

LAURIOL PLAZA, 1801 18th Street NW, Washington. Telephone: (202) 387-0035. Hours: noon–midnight daily. Cards: AE, CB, DC, MC, V. Reservations suggested. Full bar service.

Washington: Downtown
LE GAULOIS
French $$

Steady and true, always interesting and still reasonable is the French cuisine at Le Gaulois. It's as crowded as a tourist-class ship galley, and service emphasizes efficiency rather than personableness. But when the kitchen hits, it bats a home run. Appetizers are not its best course, though simple shellfish and cold vegetable dishes are generally impeccable. But look for complexity in the main dishes, perhaps the freshest and moistest fish enclosing a smidgeon of vegetable and wrapped in a light and flaky puff pastry, or a cassoulet with depth and character. I have encountered dry and tough grilled fish and a braised veal and vegetable concoction that tasted lifeless. But the rule here is a wide choice of the season's best, cooked with distinction and offered in surprising combinations. This is the restaurant for those who have a taste for French culinary professionalism, but want to pay for what is on the plate rather than on the wall or in the square footage. A Gallic bargain, not cheap but a lot of talent for the price.

LE GAULOIS, 2133 Pennsylvania Avenue NW, Washington. Telephone: (202) 466-3232. Lunch: 11:30 am–2:30 pm Monday–Friday. Dinner: 5:30 pm–11 pm Monday–Thursday; 5:30 pm–midnight Friday, Saturday. Closed Sunday. Cards: AE, MC, V. Reservations suggested. Street parking or nearby lots. Full bar service. Wheelchair access.

LA FRITURE DE PETITS POISSON BLANC (FRIED BAIT FISH)	3.50
LA BISQUE DE HOMARD (LOBSTER BISQUE)	2.95
LA CREME DE BROCCOLI (CREAM OF BROCCOLI SOUP)	2.75
LES BELONS SAUCE ECHALOTTE (BELON OYSTERS WITH SHALLOTS SAUCE)	4.95
LA TERRINE DE FRUITS DE MER AU COULIS DE TOMATES (SEA FOOD PATE WITH FRESH TOMATO SAUCE AND BASIL)	4.75
LE PARFAIT DE FOIE DE VOLAILLES AU POIVRE VERT (CHICKEN LIVER PATE WITH GREEN PEPPERCORNS)	2.75
L'ASSIETTE DE SAUMON ET TRUITE FUMES (SMOKED SALMON AND TROUT)	4.75

LES ESCARGOTS AU CHABLIS (SNAILS WITH MUSHROOMS & GARLIC BUTTER)	4.50
LES MOULES PERSILLEES (MUSSELS WITH PARSLEY BUTTER)	4.50
LA SALADE D'ENDIVES ET DE TOMATES (ENDIVE AND TOMATO SALAD)	4.25
LES CELERIS REMOULADE (CELERY ROOT WITH MUSTARD MAYONNAISE)	4.25
LA SALADE D'AVOCATS (AVOCADO SALAD)	2.75
LA SALADE DE FRUITS FRAIS (FRESH FRUIT SALAD)	3.50

* * * * * *** * * * * *

LES ECREVICES SAUTEES A L'ARMORICAINE (SAUTEED CRAY FISH IN LOBSTER SAUCE)	9.25
LES MOULES MARINIERES (MUSSELA IN WHITE WINE)	8.75
LES SHAD ROE GRILLES AU BEURRE D'ANCHOIS (GRILLED SHAD ROE WITH ANCHOVIES BUTTER)	11.50
LES QUENELLES DE BROCHET SAUCE NANTUA (PIKE DUMPLINGS IN LOBSTER SAUCE)	9.25
LA BROCHETTE DE CREVETTES, COQUILLES ST. JACQUES, ET SAUMON, SAUCE CHORON (SHRIMP, SEA SCALLOPS, AND SALMON, GRILLED ON SKEWER)	11.75
LES COQUILLES ST. JACQUES MARSEILLAISE (SEA SCALLOPS SAUTEED WITH TOMATOES, GARLIC, AND PERNOD)	9.95
LES CALAMARS AUX PETITS LEGUMES SAUCE A L'AMERICAINE (SQUID CASSEROLE WITH FRESH VEGETABLES AND LOBSTER SAUCE)	8.95

* * * * * *** * * * * *

L'ENTRECOTE DE BOEUF AU POIVRE A LA PARISIENNE (PEPPER STEAK)	10.95
LES ESCALOPINES DE VEAU CHASSEUR (VEAL SCALLOPINI WITH TOMATOES, GARLIC, MUSHROOMS, TARRAGON, AND WHITE WINE)	9.75
LE CIVET DE LAPEREAU BORDELAISE (RABBIT CASSEROLE WITH PEARL ONIONS, MUSHROOMS, BACON BITS, AND RED WINE SAUCE)	9.25
LE CASSOULET DE CASTELNAUDARY (DUCK AND LAMB CASSEROLE WITH PROK SAUSAGE AND BEANS; A SPECIALTY FROM THE SOUTH OF FRANCE)	8.95
LES RIS DE VEAU SAUTES AUX MORILLES (VEAL SWEETBREADS SAUTEED WITH MORRELS (IMPORTED MUSHROOMS), CREAM & BRANDY SAUCE)	11.50

* * * * * *** * * * * *

LA SALADE DU CHEF (CHEF SALAD)	5.50
L'AVOCAT FARCI AUX FRUITS DE MER (AVOCADO STUFFED WITH SEA FOOD)	5.95
LE SAUMON FROID SAUCE VERTE (COLD SALMON WITH HERB MAYONNAISE)	9.25

* * * * * *** * * * * *

LE MIROIR AUX CASSIS ET AUX FRUITS DE LA PASSION (BLACK CURRANT AND PASSION FRUIT MOUSSE CAKE WITH FRESH STRAWBERRY SAUCE)	2.75
LES FRAISES A LA CHANTILLY (FRESH STRAWBERRIES WITH WHIPPED CREAM	3.25

Washington: Downtown
LE JARDIN
French

$$$

With arched skylights and beautiful dusty warm colors, Le Jardin seems so delicious in ambience that you may worry the food will be bad. Sweep those worries away. I have found the food usually good, only infrequently dismal. The menu is French and though it avoids nouvelle cuisine austerity and precision, its plates look pretty, the foods arranged with an eye for balance and color. It is apparent that the chef is most comfortable with seafood. As simple a dish as scallops with dill is a delicious, creamy rendition, pungent with dill in a rich sauce coating plenty of scallops cooked exactly right. Another day the pastry-wrapped salmon with scallop mousse was fresh, moist and delicate, its crust well crisped. Le Jardin also makes a marvelous cassoulet, a treasure of lamb, pork, crackly skinned duck and spicy sausage. Tread cautiously, however, among other dishes, and be prepared for some disastrous sauces—goose was once hard and dry, venison was adequate except for a swamp of sweet sauce. To begin a meal, remember the asparagus. Or try the soups and seafood appetizers. Endings are happy. The cappuccino is even memorable, partly because, like the desserts, it is blanketed with fresh and unsweetened whipped cream.

LE JARDIN, 1113 23rd Street NW, Washington. Telephone: (202) 457-0057. Hours: 11:30 am–2 am Monday–Saturday; 10:30 am–2 am Sunday. Cards: AE, CB, DC, MC, V. Reservations suggested. Free parking at dinner in lot. Full bar service.

Washington: Downtown
LE LION D'OR ✳
French

$$$

When a French restaurant stays at the top year after year despite dashing new competitors and new fashions in food, there is good reason. At Le Lion d'Or the reason is a highly professional, experienced and yet experimental kitchen staff and a similarly competent dining room staff. And compared with the other top-echelon French restaurants these days, Le Lion d'Or is a bargain. Among the exciting experiments lately have been duck sausages, as light as quenelles and wrapped in crisp skin—superb. And fresh pigeon has been cooked to a fine juiciness and crispness, deliciously teamed with nearly melting cabbage or with wild mushrooms. Seafoods are well cared for, whether tiny scallops served cold in a julienne of vegetables with a restrained touch of coriander, the silkiest turbot in a delicate chervil cream or a whole fish stuffed with a mousse or wrapped in a pastry. It is the restraint that shows Le Lion d'Or's experience to best advantage: Salmon with red bell peppers only hints of that strong seasoning. Coriander is just a whisper. Tarragon provides an aura for medallions of lamb rather than swamping them. There are certainly missteps or dishes that are disappointingly ordinary. And despite a glamorous array of pastries, I would stick to the high and airy souffles or the piquant sorbets. I still feel fresh irritation every time the list of specials—too long to

remember and without the prices even hinted—is recited to me rather than printed for me to read. But the grand and blessedly fair-priced wine list, the continual stocking of the best and hardest-to-find ingredients and the sure touch in their preparation fix Le Lion d'Or firmly as a restaurant of excellence.

LE LION D'OR, 1150 Connecticut Avenue NW, Washington. Telephone: (202) 296-7972. Lunch: noon–2 pm Monday–Friday. Dinner: 6 pm–10 pm Monday–Saturday. Closed Sunday. Cards: AE, CB, DC, MC, V. Reservations required. Free parking lot. Full bar service. Wheelchair access. Jacket and tie required.

Les Entrées

L' escalope de veau aux morilles et truffes $22.00

Le carré d'agneau au poivre vert (2 pers.) $52.00

Le filet d' agneau roti au thym $22.00

Le Tournedos sauté à la moèlle $26.00

Les Mignonettes de filet au poire à la crème $25.00

Les rognons de veau dijonnaise $16.00

La casserole de ris de veau au porto $18.50

Le filet de volaille au foie gras
                                    et morilles noire $21.00

Les aiguillettes de canard au cassis $20.00

Le poulet roti à l' estragon $17.00

Le poulet sauté au poivre et raisins $18.00

Le lapin roti à la moutarde $16.00

Les escalopines de veau à la francaise $18.00

Le Filet de veau au ragout fin $24.00

Le Pigeon roti sauce foie gras $19.00

LE PAVILLON ✳

French   **$$$**

Except for the Rousseauesque mural in the entrance, this sedately lovely dining room doesn't suggest that you are entering a world where food is raised to fantasy, where pigeon breasts are rolled into tiny perfect ballotines and garnished with miniature batons of artichoke and zucchini flowers, where a liver-and-bacon theme is amusingly carried out with exquisite smoky grilled slices of foie gras under a tangle of equally subtle bacon. Here is food that matches the magic of anything Europe has to offer: flans and mousses of sheer velvet, afloat with slivers of shad roe or other seasonal fish, the lightest of little puff pastry boxes with a treasure of wild mushrooms, fresh basil leaves and tomatoes. Dinners are fixed price at $50 to $100, though they may be ordered a la carte, and run four to six courses, each one a little jewel, the most perfect of meats and seafoods and bits of vegetable in a precious setting. The wine list is an extraordinary resource, particularly rich in burgundies but inordinately tempting no matter what vintage, region or price range you choose. It all fits at Le Pavillon: the simple luxury of the trappings, the well oiled service and, most important, food that is clearly high art.

LE PAVILLON, 1050 Connecticut Avenue NW, Washington. Telephone: (202) 833-3846. Lunch: 11:45 am–2 pm Monday–Friday. Dinner: 6:45 pm–10 pm Monday–Saturday; 6:45 pm until closing Sunday. Cards: AE, CB, DC, MC, V. Reservations required. Valet parking at dinner. Full bar service. Wheelchair access. Jacket and tie required.

Washington: Georgetown
MADURAI ✳
Indian (Vegetarian) $

The idea of an Indian vegetarian restaurant sounds like a tune with few notes: mushrooms with curry powder, peas with curry powder, cauliflower with curry powder. At Madurai though, you can expect no two dishes to taste alike, have the same color or even very similar textures. It is food that challenges the senses to recognize, to unravel the layers of flavor. Dosais, which come in five versions, deserve special attention, being thin, crisp rice-based pancakes that make French crêpes seem simple-minded. Curries are less reliable than the dosais (particularly the gobi alu and saag paneer), yet navratan curry, said to be made of nine vegetables, and full of sweet fragrances and minglings of spices, is the single best dish. Mushroom curry with tomatoes and onions and vegetable kofta curry are also fine, intriguing mixes of seasonings. Breads are a highlight of Indian cooking— and a highlight of Madurai. If breads are the high point, desserts are the low. Even without dessert, though, there is little danger of leaving Madurai hungry. The portions are large, the food invites you to nibble and to combine and taste again until you have exceeded your capacity. At Madurai you are likely to feel you have been served a lot of satisfaction for relatively little money.

MADURAI, 3318 M Street NW, Washington. Telephone: (202) 333-0997. Brunch: noon–4 pm Sunday. Lunch: noon–4 pm Monday–Saturday. Dinner: 5 pm–10 pm Monday–Sunday. Cards: AE, CB, DC, MC, V. Reservations suggested. Street parking. Full bar service. Non-smoking area.

Washington: Downtown
MAISON BLANCHE
French

$$$

The kitchen is always venturing into something new at Maison Blanche. For its best efforts see the daily specials and those dishes noted to be house specialties. There might be oysters wrapped in spinach on a lovely saffron sauce, or warm treviso lettuce bathed in hazelnut oil and tossed with shrimp. The menu has even listed antelope. But the classics also are often outstanding, whether lobster bisque—probably the best in town—or veal chop smothered in the season's wild mushrooms and cream. Ask for advice; the waiters can warn you when the duckling is not at its best. The wine list is long and enticing, with good values sprinkled among the heavyweights. Dessert is a gorgeous display of highly professional pastries, and in case you are indecisive, a plate that presents a miniature version of the best. Maison Blanche holds firmly to the upper rungs among Washington's French restaurants.

MAISON BLANCHE, 1725 F Street NW, Washington. Telephone: (202) 842-0070. Lunch: 11:45 am–2:30 pm Monday–Friday. Dinner: 6 pm–11 pm Monday–Friday; 6 pm–11:30 pm Saturday. Closed Sunday. Cards: AE, CB, DC, MC, V. Reservations suggested. Free valet parking at dinner. Full bar service. Wheelchair access. Jacket and tie required.

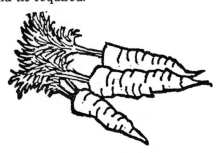

Washington: Upper Northwest
MALABAR
Indian $

Malabar has become one of the most treasured neighbors of upper Wisconsin Avenue, for it is a quiet, unaffected Indian restaurant where prices are low and the food good, though intermittently. Not at all fancy, it is modestly decorated with Indian prints and pierced metal lanterns. And the a la carte menu allows you to put together a light meal or a banquet. Start with chicken tikka, an appetizer of two drumsticks coated with spices and grilled to a crusty finish. You could make a meal of appetizers— kebabs, samosas, pakoras and masala dosa (though this latter one needs doctoring with chutneys to spark it). And maybe you should stop there, for main dishes are more variable. When in doubt, stick to curries. And by all means try the breads.

MALABAR, 4934 Wisconsin Avenue NW, Washington. Telephone: (202) 363-8900. Lunch: 11:30 am–2:30 pm Monday–Friday. Dinner: 5:30 pm–10:30 pm Sunday–Thursday; 5:30 pm–11 pm Friday, Saturday. Cards: AE, CB, DC, MC, V. Reservations suggested. Street parking. Full bar service. Non-smoking area.

Appetizers

Samosa — a thin triangular pastry filled with vegetables and
deep fried 95

Masala Dosa — a type of pancake made with batter of ground lentils
and rice filled with potatoes and spices 2.50

Keema Dosa — pancake stuffed with ground beef and peas 2.95

Pokora — deep fried vegetable in batter 1.50

Tikka Kebab — tiny chunks of lamb mixed with spices and broiled 2.25

Chicken Tikka — boneless chicken with spices and broiled 2.95

Soup — Mulligatawny 2.95

Entrees

Lamb

Roghan Josh — a special Indian preparation 8.95

Lamb Dopiaja — chunks of lamb cooked with spices 9.50

Lamb Biryani — with special Indian spices and herbs 9.95

Lamb Vandaloo 9.95

Goat Curry — on the bone 8.95

Chicken

Tandoori Murgh — half spring chicken, marinated in spices 7.95

Shah Jehani Curry — tradition Shah Jehani style chicken
cooked in curry 7.95

Saag Chicken — chicken cooked with spinach and spices 7.50

Chicken Biryani — a festive dish with special Indian
spices and herbs 8.50

Beef

Bhuna Gost — chunks of beef cooked with spices 7.95

Saag Gost — chunks of beef cooked with spinach 7.50

Shahi Korma — beef cooked with spices and herbs 7.50

Keema Matar — ground beef exquisitely curried with spices 7.50

From The Sea

Fish Curry — chef's special curry 8.50

Shrimp Curry — shrimp curried with spices and herbs 10.95

Shrimp Biryani — with special Indian spices and herbs 11.95

Fried Fish — Malabar style (HOT) 6.95

A choice of environments is what the Market Inn offers: a party-lover's room with music and a friendly crowd, or a dim and quiet booth lit by red globes and away from the path of the dining crowd. Nice choice. And a nice choice of seafoods fills four pages and a couple of daily sheets with lobsters from a tank, crabs, scallops, oysters, fish fillets and a half-dozen combination platters, plus there are a few grilled meats. There are even nine soups—not bad, the soups. Clam chowder tastes of cream and clams, not the insides of cans. And snapper soup is harsh and strong at the first spoonful, better as you adjust to it. Not great cooking here, but serviceable. The fish fillets are cooked dry, but you can get a nice oyster dressing on them. Fried shrimp are better than average, but not great. It is one of those seafood restaurants that specializes in everything from Greek salad to carrot cake. Choice is its strong suit.

MARKET INN, 200 E Street SW, Washington. Telephone: (202) 554-2100. Hours: 11 am–2 am Monday–Saturday; 4 pm–midnight Sunday. Cards: AE, CB, DC, MC, V. Reservations suggested. Free valet parking. Full bar service. Wheelchair access.

APPETIZERS

Hot Hors d'Oeuvres
Deep Fried Jumbo Shrimps, Scallops,
Oysters and Crab Cake Balls
For Two - 9.95

Cold Seafood Appetizer
Jumbo Shrimp, Oysters, Clams,
Crab and Lobster Meat
For Two - 9.95

Long Island Oyster Cocktail 4.75   Fresh Lump Crab Meat Cocktail 6.75
Cherrystone Clam Cocktail 4.75   Jumbo Shrimp Cocktail 6.25
Lobster Meat Cocktail 6.75   Clams Casino or Oysters Casino (5) 5.25
Alaskan King Crabmeat Cocktail 8.75   Hot or Cold Spiced Shrimp 6.25
La Damie Douraine D'Escargots 5.75
Oysters Rockefeller, New Orleans Style (5) 5.25
Baked Mushroom Caps stuffed with Oyster Dressing 2.95
Fried Potato Skins (with Sour Cream) 2.75
—————— STEAMED SOFT CLAMS (10) 4.25 ——————

Famous Soups Made Daily at Market Inn
Prices are Per Cup - Bowls are Double Cup Price

Try our Fresh Soup Du Jour 1.75

She Crab Soup - Charleston Style 2.50
Snapper Turtle Soup 2.50   New England Clam Chowder 2.00
Baked French Style Onion Soup 1.75   Vichysoisse - French Style 1.95
Crab Gumbo - New Orleans Style 2.50   Lobster Bisque 2.75
Stewed Oysters with Half & Half (Bowl only) 4.75

COLD SEAFOOD PLATTERS & SALAD

3 WAY COMBINATION SEAFOOD SALAD - Lobster, Shrimp and Crabmeat **13.75**
LOBSTER SALAD 11.50   SHRIMP SALAD 9.75
FRESH BAY CRABMEAT SALAD 10.50
CHEF SEAFOOD SALAD 9.50
AVOCADO - Stuffed with your choice of
SHRIMP, LOBSTER or CRAB SALAD 13.75
CHEF'S SALAD 7.95   JOHNNY THE GREEK SALAD 8.25
Above served with a Variety of Appetizing Garnishes
HEARTS OF LETTUCE 1.75

VEGETABLES
FRESH MUSHROOM CAPS - Sauteed in Butter **2.25**
BROCCOLI or ASPARAGUS HOLLANDAISE 2.25
FRENCH FRIED ONION RINGS 2.25

DESSERTS
Chocolate Mousse Cake 2.75   Piña Colada Cake 2.75
Rich Chocolate Cake   Freshly Made Carrot Cake
Amaretto Cake   Key Lime Pie   Deep South Pecan Pie
2.25

Apple Pie 1.75   Ice Cream 1.50   Mother's All-Natural Cheese Cake 2.50
Old Fashioned Strawberry Shortcake - Made with Fresh Strawberries 2.50
Parfaits - All Flavors 2.75
We will gladly warm Pies and Cakes upon request

QUICHE - SANDWICHES - EGGS
QUICHE OF THE DAY 6.75   MIXED SEAFOOD OMELET 7.95   EGGS BENEDICT
STEAK SANDWICH 7.75   LARGE CLUB SANDWICH 6.95
MARKET BURGER - Try It 5.95   CRAB CAKE 7.25

BIRTHDAY CAKES AVAILABLE UPON REQUEST 7.50

93

Washington: Downtown
MARRAKESH
Moroccan $$

Dinner at Washington's first Moroccan restaurant hap-
pens in a great bazaar of a room, with a many-course
meal delivered by kneeling waiters and punctuated by
three handwashings. One course is bisteeya, the Moroccan
national dish, made of chicken, custardy egg, parsley
and nuts wrapped in phyllo dough and topped with
confectioners' sugar and cinnamon—a blend of flavors
both startling and irresistible. Best main dishes are
spicy chicken with cumin and lamb cubed, stewed with
honey and tossed with whole almonds. Dinner may take
hours, but there's nothing else like it.

MARRAKESH, 617 New York Avenue NW, Washington.
Telephone: (202) 393-9393. Dinner: 6 pm–11 pm
Monday–Friday; 5:30 pm–11 pm Saturday; 5 pm–11
pm Sunday. No credit cards. Reservations required.
Valet parking. Full bar service. Wheelchair access.

Washington: Downtown
MEL KRUPIN'S
American $$$

Newcomers may not understand the reverence for Mel
Krupin's, since it is best loved for its past. Anybody who
tends to slip and call it Duke's understands, even
though Duke's has revived as its strongest competition.
Mel's is the offspring, the second generation, the carrier
of the tradition, the tradition being reliable and solid he-
man fare. At Mel's a waiter in black tie will serve you
herring and gossip about the track or the game. Your
chairs will be comfortable, your table topped with linen,
your view dressed with etched glass and soft velvety
fabrics. But nobody winces if you start your meal with a
garlicky dill pickle or fill up on homemade onion rolls or

salt sticks. At Mel Krupin's healthy doesn't mean yogurt and low-cholesterol alternatives, but chicken soup with a big fat matzo ball or a thick and crusty and very fine steak that will keep up your strength. And daily specials are the same every week, summer or winter. Monday stuffed cabbage, for instance, Thursday corned beef and cabbage, Saturday duck with a lot of sweetness in the apple-raisin stuffing but none of that Frenchified orange sauce for this crisp and juicy bird. Look for heartiness and plain stuff: fresh fish, plump oysters and clams, chicken or beef in a pot, roast beef. High prices, yes, and overcooking sometimes, but good old reliable food, with large baked potatoes unmodernized by foil, a huge portion of some vegetable like creamed spinach, and dessert that specializes in being mile-high. Look for subtleties, intricacy and delicacy elsewhere. Mel Krupin's is for meat-and-potatoes men (and women), even when they have switched to fish.

MEL KRUPIN'S, 1120 Connecticut Avenue NW, Washington. Telephone: (202) 331-7000. Hours: 11:30 am–10:30 pm Monday–Friday. Lunch: noon–3 pm Saturday. Dinner: 5 pm–10:30 pm Saturday. Closed Sunday. Cards: AE, CB, DC, MC, V. Reservations suggested. Valet parking at dinner only. Full bar service. Wheelchair access. Jacket required.

Washington: Upper Northwest
MIKADO
Japanese $$

All is grace at Mikado, a small Japanese restaurant where kimonoed waitresses with lilting voices serve lacquered bowls of precisely arranged sushi and sashimi, small pottery dishes of unctuous broiled eel that looks lacquered with soy sauce, small iron kettles of broth afloat with meats and vegetables enveloped in sweet spicy smells. The best sampling, unless you can arrange a group visit, is a special dinner of suki-nabe or teriyaki for one, or shabu shabu for two. These start with fragrant clear or opaque soup, go on to raw fish or tempura, then to pickles or sesame-and-lemon-dressed salad before the main course. All to be accompanied with warm sake and an air of serenity. Mikado was the second of Washington's Japanese restaurants, and has slipped well down the list as competition has increased. But the opening of its sushi bar has brought a new energy.

MIKADO, 4707 Wisconsin Avenue NW, Washington. Telephone: (202) 244-1740. Lunch: 11:30 am–2 pm Tuesday–Saturday. Dinner: 5:30 pm–10 pm Tuesday–Sunday. Closed Monday. Cards: AE, CB, DC, MC, V. Reservations suggested. Street parking. Full bar service.

Washington: Downtown
MONTPELIER ROOM
Continental $$$

If price is no object, the Montpelier Room serves well as a personal lunch club. The dining room is a setting of grandeur, royal blue and gold everywhere, the tables set with luxurious china and silver ornaments and not one but two long-stemmed roses in each bud vase. Service is well oiled, with an eye kept on your needs from a discreet distance. All is hushed. Everything is polished. The menu is a parade of costly ingredients and traditional Continental dishes with something for everyone and no offense to any sensibilities. Nor are there surprises, adventures; this is what is known as hotel fare. It can be very good; on occasion it is superb. Perfectly fresh sea trout grilled to its juiciest, with a crusty, buttery surface, is accompanied with garlicky fresh green beans and parsley potatoes. Crab au gratin brings giant pearls of crab in a soft, buttery cream with just enough pimiento. But given the fact that the best of the food is plain food, the prices are outlandish, all the more so when the kitchen slips into overcooking and underseasoning. The wine list is tantalizing in its depth, but the prices spoil one's appetite. At dessert time, trays are wheeled to the table, everything expertly made and beautiful, and the rice pudding is memorable. Coffee is served and refilled from your china pot. Nice touches. But at the price it costs, one is paying for individuality as well as comfort, and at the Montpelier you get only comfort, though certainly enough of that.

MONTPELIER ROOM, 15th and M Streets NW (in the Madison Hotel), Washington. Telephone: (202) 862-1600. Breakfast: 7 am–10:30 am Monday–Friday. Brunch: 11 am–3 pm Sunday. Lunch: noon–2:30 pm Monday–Friday. Dinner: 6 pm–10:30 pm Monday–Friday; 6 pm–10 pm Saturday, Sunday. Cards: AE, CB, DC, MC, V. Reservations suggested. Valet parking or garage parking. Full bar service. Wheelchair access. Jacket and tie required.

Washington: Georgetown
MORTON'S OF CHICAGO ✳
Steakhouse

$$$

Morton's has become Washington's best steakhouse, serving thick, well-aged, juicy meat as crusty and as rare as you could want—with superb accompaniments as well. The round loaf of bread is warm and crusty, smoked salmon is outstanding, hash browns are crisp and buttery, spinach and mushrooms are freshly cooked. But salad dressings tend to be heavy-handed and tomatoes are pallid, and Morton's proves again that anything but boiling or steaming ruins a lobster, for its is broiled. Then there is the chocolate souffle, light and airy but asking for better chocolate flavor. Still, you're really there for a monumental steak or a stunning veal chop in a comfortable, clubby dining room.

MORTON'S OF CHICAGO, 3251 Prospect Street NW, Washington. Telephone: (202) 342-6258. Dinner: 5:30 pm–10:30 pm Monday–Saturday. Closed Sunday. Cards: AE, CB, DC, MC, V. No reservations after 7 pm. Nearby parking lot. Full bar service. Wheelchair access. Jacket and tie suggested.

Washington: Downtown
MR. K'S
Chinese

$$$

If it's Chinese food you want but European elegance you crave, Mr. K's is your restaurant. The dining room is soft and plush, a cave of velvet and etched glass, with space to spare. Service is full of flourishes, from hot towels to palate-cleansing sherbet to coffee service that looks Dansk-designed. The food is good, and in some cases—such as the shark's fin soup—wonderful. In others, such as stir-fried lamb with scallions, it is creditable but no more so than elsewhere. Szechuan dishes just suggest hotness, and oversalting has been a problem with milder dishes. In general, though, Mr. K's carries its luxuriousness through to the kitchen, with giant shrimps gently cooked, daiquiris made from fresh kiwis, quail and frogs' legs and bird's nests in the larder. But beware of waiters who encourage you to order more or in larger quantity or to leave the choices up to them—food and wine prices edged up here this past year.

MR. K'S, 2121 K Street NW, Washington. Telephone: (202) 331-8868. Hours: 11:30 am–11 pm Monday–Thursday; 11:30 am–11:30 pm Friday; 12:30 pm–11:30 pm Saturday; 12:30 pm–11 pm Sunday. Cards: AE, CB, DC, MC, V. Reservations suggested. Free valet parking at dinner or parking lot. Full bar service. Wheelchair access. Non-smoking area. Jacket and tie required.

Washington: Upper Northwest
MRS. SIMPSON'S
American $$

Reliably adorable is Mrs. Simpson's, a small restaurant
that serves as a gem of a museum for romantic English
memorabilia, for Wally was the Mrs. Simpson honored
here. As for the food, it has gone through several
waxings and wanings. The style is new American, a kind
of younger sister to 209½ without the panache. The
menu is always clever, the ingredients lean hard on
freshness, and by and large the results are good. The
menu, in the 209½ style, is short. And it changes
frequently enough to satisfy the neighbors who have
made it a regular stop. But what can I say? One season
it's good, one season it slips. One dish works, another
doesn't. It's a nice little restaurant worth watching.

MRS. SIMPSON'S, 2915 Connecticut Avenue NW,
Washington. Telephone: (202) 332-8300. Brunch:
11:30 am–2:30 pm Sunday. Lunch: 11:30 am–2:30 pm
Monday–Friday. Dinner: 6 pm–10:30 pm Monday–
Thursday; 6 pm–11:30 pm Friday, Saturday; 6 pm–
10:30 pm Sunday. Cards: AE, CB, DC, MC, V. Reser-
vations suggested. Street parking. Full bar service.
Wheelchair access.

entrees for winter

veal scallopini layered with eggplant and fontina   **12.95**

swordfish steak au poivre
  *swordfish is grilled with peppercorns and
  dressed with a sweet pepper puree*   **12.95**

fresh mussels marinara with linguini   **9.95**

shrimp sauteed with snow peas and scallions   **12.95**

lamb chops grilled with oregano
  with pommery mustard   **(3)**   **11.95**   **(4)**   **14.95**

fillet mignon with sun dried tomatoes and onion rings
  or bearnaise sauce   **15.95**

calf's liver with mustard-chive sauce   **10.95**

tonight's pasta primavera   *please inquire*

mixed seafood sampler: *at market*
  *two grilled fish accompanied
  by devilled shrimp and baby crab cake*

desserts

  pecan pastry with warm caramel sauce   3.50

  sour cream chocolate cake with heavy cream   3.50

  prunes noel coward, *served with heavy cream*   2.95

  lemon meringue mousse   2.95

Washington: Downtown
NATIONAL GALLERY OF ART
CASCADE AND TERRACE CAFES
American   **$**

There are four places to eat in the National Gallery: a cafeteria and the Cascade Cafe on the bottom floor of the main building, the Garden Cafe a flight up and the Terrace Cafe two flights up in the East Building. I'd opt for the Terrace Cafe. Its advantage is that it is away from foot traffic, yet is in full view of the Calder mobile, the skylights and the Rodin statuary. The Cascade Cafe's advantage is, obviously enough, the wonderful waterfall that provides its backdrop. The menus of the cafes are nearly identical; the food will neither offend nor excite anybody. The sleeper among the desserts is a hot fudge sundae made with Haagen Dazs ice cream and a dense bittersweet fudge sauce. It would offer a happy ending to any outing.

NATIONAL GALLERY CAFES, 600 Constitution Avenue NW, Washington. Telephone: (202) 347-9401. Cascade Cafe and Garden Cafe hours: 11 am–3:30 pm Monday–Saturday; noon–6 pm Sunday. Terrace Cafe hours: 11 am–4:30 pm Monday–Saturday; noon–6 pm Sunday. Cafeteria hours: 10 am–4 pm Monday–Saturday; noon–6 pm Sunday. No credit cards. No reservations. Nearby parking lot. Beer and wine only. Wheelchair access. Non-smoking area in cafeteria.

Washington: Downtown
NEW ORLEANS EMPORIUM ✻
American   **$$**

The menu here is nearly all seafood, and in New Orleans style the categories are simple (oysters, crawfish, shrimp, crab, fish, etc.) and the descriptions unelaborate (etouffee, creole, boil, remoulade and such). The blackboard lists daily specials, but there is no rhyme nor reason to which are best. Oysters on the half-shell are brought in from the Gulf. Or you can drink your oyster in a shot glass, submerged in peppered vodka or gin. If you like them cooked, try the oysters commander, buried under a thick onion-spiked stuffing. For other appetizers look into the Cajun popcorn, or try redfish or catfish beignets. Naturally there are gumbo, crawfish bisque and turtle soup, fortunately available as a trio of demitasse cupfuls. After such appetizers and the basket of crunchy hush puppies and hot biscuits—flavored with jalapeños, peppered cured meat or blueberries—main dishes might seem superfluous. But then you would miss the blackened redfish. In all, the New Orleans Emporium buys excellent seafood—the shrimps are a revelation for anyone used to frozen ones; the crab is in snowy lumps; the fish has been impeccably fresh. Brunch offers several poached-egg surprises. Finally, dessert is not to be ignored here. The bread pudding is thick, dense, sweet, rich, brandied and marvelous. The chicory coffee, regular and decaffeinated, is served traditionally, with plenty of milk. I have skipped the environment—it is not the important part. The Emporium is cute, all tiles and plain wood, clattery and busy. It is not the place to go for a romantic evening, but certainly for good fun and food worthy of New Orleans' reputation.

NEW ORLEANS EMPORIUM, 2477 18th Street NW, Washington. Telephone: (202) 328-3421. Brunch: 11:30 am–3 pm Saturday, Sunday. Lunch: 11:30 am–2:30 pm Sunday–Thursday. Dinner: 5:30 pm–11 pm Sunday–Thursday; 5:30 pm–midnight Friday, Saturday. Cards: AE, CB, DC, MC, V. Reservations suggested. Nearby parking lot. Full bar service.

The emphasis is on new American food in the Mayflower's tiny and ambitious new Nicholas restaurant. The menu is full of fashionable ingredients—red bell peppers, green peppercorns, raspberry vinegar, enoki mushrooms. And inventive dishes combine flavors of Europe and Asia with America's best resources: crab meat, swordfish, Maine lobster, red snapper, Wisconsin duck, rack of lamb, fillet of beef. Appetizers are beautifully garnished with tomato roses and dabs of caviar, or with tiny pickled vegetables or tropical fruits. They decorate marinated salmon and scallops or tuna tartare, scallop-stuffed ravioli or lobster in beurre blanc, foie gras both hot and cold. Main courses might be crisp-skinned nearly boned and flattened pigeon, or the fashionable blackened redfish. Lobster is teamed with dill and cucumbers, salmon with a bouquet of enoki mushrooms. In a room of pale colors and crystal chandeliers, not as imaginative as the menu but certainly comfortable, Nicholas is pioneering with new dishes fashioned from outstanding ingredients. And the endings—maple souffle, creme brulee, brioche bread pudding or strawberry-covered meringue—are high points of a dinner that most likely has already impressed you.

NICHOLAS, 1127 Connecticut Avenue NW (in the Mayflower Hotel), Washington. Telephone: (202) 347-8900. Lunch: 11:30 am–2:30 pm Monday–Friday. Dinner: 6 pm–10 pm daily. Cards: AE, CB, DC, MC, V. Reservations suggested. Valet parking for dinner only. Full bar service. Wheelchair access. Jacket and tie required.

APPETIZERS

Marinated SALMON and SEA SCALLOPS, Green Peppercorns and Lime 7.50

Tartare of Fresh TUNA with Olive Oil and Chives 6.50

Terrine of Muscovy DUCK, Accompanied with Pickled Vegetables 4.75

SCALLOP RAVIOLIS, Thyme Butter Sauce 7.00

Bouquet of LOBSTER, Served Warm in Vermouth Sauce 9.50

Fresh DUCK FOIE GRAS Sauteed, Fresh Coriander Sauce 12.00

SOUPS

Cream of GRILLED EGGPLANT, with Bell Pepper and Sesame 4.25

Double PHEASANT CONSOMME, Flavored with Orange, Ginger and Tomato 4.50

SALADS

Fresh Seasonal Greens tossed with Almond Oil and Raspberry Vinegar 4.25

LUMP CRABMEAT and CRAYFISH Salad "Nicholas" 7.50

ENTREES

Steamed Filet of SALMON, Riesling Sauce and Enoki Mushrooms 17.50

Grilled SWORDFISH STEAK, Fresh Tomato and Herb Sauce 18.00

Fricasse of MAINE LOBSTER, with Dill and Cucumbers 23.50

Sauteed Filet of RED SNAPPER, Puree of Two Peppers, Lime Butter Sauce 18.50

Medallions of VEAL with Green Peppercorn Sauce and Grapefruit 21.00

Breast of Wisconsin DUCK, Roasted Pink, with a Cabernet Sauce 17.25

SWEETBREADS Sauteed with Fresh Coriander and Ginger Cream Sauce 16.50

RACK OF LAMB with Wild Mushrooms, Artichoke Hearts, and Tarragon Sauce 22.00

FILET OF BEEF Sauteed, Sweet Onion and Stone Ground Mustard 20.00

DESSERTS

CHEESE Selection of the Day

with our Suggested Wines 8.75   with Seasonal Fruits 4.25

CHOCOLATE MOUSSE on Pistachio Cream 5.00

BRIOCHE PUDDING and Lingonberry Sauce 4.00

MAPLE BOURBON SOUFFLE (Allow 20 Minutes) 5.25

Meringue with Marinated STRAWBERRIES and Cracked Black Peppercorn 5.50

This little restaurant has new high prices that it sometimes lives up to. Nora's salads are wonderful, its
vegetables standouts, but both appetizers and entrees
are sometimes good, sometimes not. Fish dishes usually
are excellent; sometimes the pastas are, too, but the
meats are less dependable. Exception: at lunch, fine
chopped steak topped with stilton-port butter. Stars
among the desserts are the house-made ice creams and
the truly beautiful bittersweet chocolate mousse.

NORA, 2132 Florida Avenue NW, Washington. Telephone: (202) 462-5143. Lunch: noon–2:30 pm Monday–
Friday. Dinner: 6 pm–10 pm Monday–Thursday; 6 pm–
10:30 pm Friday, Saturday. Closed Sunday. No credit
cards. Reservations suggested. Street parking. Full bar
service. Wheelchair access.

First Courses

Tomato-Carrot Soup 3.50
Nora's Paté 5.00
Chicken Liver Mousse 6.00
  with black truffles
Fresh Asparagus 6.00
  with lemon mustard
Celeri Root Remoulade 5.00
  and Carrot Salad

Maine Smoked Trout 6.00
  with sour cream horseradish sauce
Smoked Tuna Shrimp Sturgeon 7.00
  with caviar and pickled ginger
Pork Rillettes 5.00
  with toast
Mexican Sea Scallop Salad 7.00
  with chilies and cilantro

Main Courses

Homemade Saffron Fettuccine - served with artichoke, sundried tomatoes, ~18.00
  peppers, and fresh herb sauce, sprinkled with feta cheese
Rabbit Curry - braised with fragrant curry spices and yogurt, ~19.00
  served with cinnamon poppy seed bread, homemade fig
  chutney, coriander-chili relish, and cumin seed raita
Pompano and Shrimp in Parchment with roasted red peppers,~ 23.00
  crabmeat, asparagus, and lemon herb butter
Beef Liver - sautéed and served with sherry vinegar sauce, butternut ~18.00
  squash purée, and roasted Jerusalem artichokes
Veal Loin Steak - sautéed and served with calvados sauce, broiled ~23.00
  shiitake mushrooms, baby carrots, and steamed broccoli
Florida Swordfish - broiled and served with tomato-basil ~23.00
  beurre blanc, purple beans, sugar snap peas, and salsify
California Hen - boneless breast stuffed with goat cheese and ~19.00
  fresh herbs served with tarragon mustard sauce,
  baby cauliflower, and brussel sprouts

Salads

Spinach and Mushrooms 5.00
  with feta cheese dressing
Mixed greens 5.00
  with blackberry vinaigrette
Mache Lettuce and Goat Cheese 7.00
  with lemon extra virgin
  olive oil dressing

Arugola Salad with anchovies, capers, 5.00
  tomatoes, and sherry vinaigrette
Belgian Endive, Watercress, 6.00
  Enoki Mushrooms with tamari
  sesame oil
Baby Lettuces 5.00
  with balsamic vinaigrette

Homemade Desserts

Rehrücken - chocolate almond cake 4.00
French Bittersweet Chocolate 5.00
  Mousse with walnut sauce
Apple Pie 5.00
  with vanilla ice cream
Mixed Berries with cream 7.00
Vermont Cheddar Cheese 5.00
  with apple

Raspberry Surprise 7.00
Caramel Ice Cream with toasted 4.00
  almonds and crème anglaise
Banana Ice Cream 4.00
  with chocolate kahlua sauce
Blood Orange and Kiwi Sorbets 4.00
  with strawberry sauce

Washington: Downtown
OLD EBBITT GRILL
American

$$

The new Old Ebbitt is around the corner from the original, in what was one of Washington's grand old movie theaters. And, like the Clyde's operations before it, no expense has been spared in the furnishing. The walls are mahogany, the curtains lace; the ceilings are muraled and stenciled, and the green leathery and velvety booths are rendered private by etched glass dividers. What isn't marble or gilt is brass. The long bars are watched over by stuffed animal heads. There 200 table seats plus 75 stools at two bars and an oyster bar; still there is room to spare. No culinary trend is spared. Wines are connected to a Cruvinet system, allowing fine wines to be sold by the glass without the risk of spoiling the leftovers. The menu changes daily, and everything from pasta to ice cream is made on the premises. Pheasant and trout are procured fresh from their

BAKED SCROD PESCADU 9.95
Fresh scrod baked with lemon slices and tomatoes, served with beurre blanc.

CHICKEN PAILLARD 9.50
Boneless breast of chicken marinated in olive oil, lemon and garlic, then grilled over live coals.

FETTUCINE WITH CHICKEN PRIMA VERA 10.25
Tender strips of chicken tossed with fresh vegetables and fettucine in a cream sauce with parmesan cheese and garlic.

LINGUINE WITH SEAFOOD 11.95
Shrimp, scallops, squid and mussels sauteed in butter with garlic and tomatoes, finished with a saffron cream sauce.

STRAW AND HAY 10.25
Green and white pasta tossed with parmesan, mushrooms, peas, prosiutto and onions.

CANNELONI DI CASA 10.95
Homemade pasta with spinach, mortadella ham and four cheeses baked in a cream sauce.

respective ranches, and salmon is said to be flown in from Alaska. The grill is said to be a special charcoal burner. From Italy's fried mozzarella to Hungary's goulash to Greek-style shrimp with feta, the world is represented. And like the Clyde's that came before it, the best of the Old Ebbitt is its hamburger. Old Ebbitt is a scintillating new dining room, beautiful right down to the rest rooms, which you should not miss seeing. Its menu sounds fashionable and fun. But it doesn't wear as well as it looks on the hanger. It serves fair food, though at fair enough prices which may keep its fans trying.

OLD EBBITT GRILL, 675 15th Street NW, Washington. Telephone: (202) 347-4801. Breakfast: 7 am–11 am Monday–Friday; 8 am–11 am Saturday. Brunch: 10 am–3 pm Sunday. Lunch: noon–3 pm Monday–Friday. Dinner: 4 pm–2 am Sunday–Thursday; 4 pm–3 am Friday, Saturday. Cards: AE, CB, DC, MC, V. Reservations suggested. Street parking, garage parking or valet parking. Full bar service.

T-BONE STEAK 15.95
Grilled over live charcoal, served with Old Ebbitt steak sauce.

TROUT PARMESAN 9.95
Fresh Virginia trout dipped in egg batter and parmesan cheese, deep fried and topped with a ribbon of hollandaise.

EGGS BENEDICT 7.25

GRILLED SWORDFISH 14.75
Grilled over live coals and topped with a chardonnay mustard sauce.

ROAST LEG OF LAMB 12.95
Spit-roasted over live charcoal. Served with roast potato and vegetable

STEAMED SCALLOPS ORIENTAL 11.95
Nantucket scallops marinated in soy sauce, ginger and sesame oil and steamed with vegetables.

BEEF STEW 9.75
Tender pieces of beef cooked with vegetables and potato served with crusty bread.

Washington: Georgetown
OLD EUROPE
German
$

Old Europe practically needs its own tourist bureau to keep the public informed of its festivals. There is the asparagus festival and Berliner Weissbier time, the game festival and the May wine festival. There is always something to celebrate, and that gives you an idea of what fun the restaurant can be. It looks accurately Middle European, its walls covered with ornately framed old-fashioned paintings. Evenings, there is piano music. Waitresses are cheerful, amusing and terribly efficient. And, as one expects in a German restaurant, the food is heavy and filling, and would be so even were it not served in such huge portions. Two of the greatest pleasures at Old Europe are alcoholic. German beers are, of course, plentiful. And the wine list indulges all one's whims for Rhines and Mosels in abundance, with fair prices and an uncommonly good choice of half bottles. Food, of course, is central; choose dishes that are from the peasant rather than the urban repertoire. To start, the wurstsalat or a soup (especially cold fruit soup in season) are well made. Continue to pigs' knuckles or wursts rather than veal dishes, which taste more like peasant food than they are meant to. Dumplings, sauerkraut and red cabbage are good enough to patch the disappointment. For dessert, concentrate on cheese-cake, which the kitchen does superbly, far better than the apple strudel or apple pie. Be sure to take advantage of the festivals' special dishes.

OLD EUROPE, 2434 Wisconsin Avenue NW, Washington. Telephone: (202) 333-7600. Lunch: 11:30 am–3 pm Monday–Saturday. Dinner: 5 pm–10:30 pm Monday–Thursday; 5 pm–midnight Friday, Saturday; 12:30 pm–10 pm Sunday. Cards: AE, CB, DC, MC, V. Reservations suggested. Street parking. Full bar service. Wheelchair access.

Washington: Downtown
OMEGA ✳
Latin American

$$

Omega is a tradition in Washington. It is the longest-running Cuban-restaurant bargain in the city. The setting is pure nonentity, with Formica tables on bare floors and a few lonely pictures on the walls, but all lately upgraded and expanded. The service is just as spare, but generally rapid, for this is a restaurant that copes with crowds. There is no sparing on the food. Fried squid as an appetizer—in a fragile haze of a crust—could serve as a main course. The real main courses are enough to feed a table, particularly with the platter of rice and bowl of black beans. The menu includes the standards: paella, ropa vieja, masitas de puerco, lomo saltado, rabbit, cuttlefish and cod, as well as very good golden soup-stews known as asopaos. The menu is in both Spanish and English, so that families waiting in line or for their dinners can pass the time with a language lesson. With all of the Adams-Morgan neighborhood's new restaurants, Omega retains its legendary attraction.

OMEGA, 1858 Columbia Road NW, Washington. Telephone: (202) 462-1732. Hours: noon–10 pm Tuesday–Sunday; noon–11 pm Friday, Saturday. Closed Monday. Cards: AE, CB, DC, MC, V. No reservations. Street parking. Full bar service. Wheelchair access.

**PAVILLION AT THE
OLD POST OFFICE
International**   **$ $**

There are two ways to go at the Pavillion: Pick and
choose among the food stands or sit down at one of the
five full-service restaurants. For value, try the stands;
the ethnic stands, particularly, serve interesting choices
at low prices. As for the restaurants, their food tends to
be pedestrian, though the Hunan attains authenticity
and some pleasant surprises in its beautiful contemporary
dining room. Otherwise, you have a choice of ordinary
pub food, ordinary French food or ordinary seafood in
an extraordinary transformation of the handsome old
post office building.

PAVILLION AT THE OLD POST OFFICE, 1100
Pennsylvania Avenue NW, Washington. CAFE MAXIME
and AMERICAN BISTRO, Telephone: (202) 289-
8464. Hours: 11:30 am–10:30 pm Monday–Thursday;
11:30 am–11 pm Friday, Saturday; noon–7 pm Sunday.
Cards: AE, MC, V. BLOSSOMS, Telephone: (202)
371-1838. Hours: 11 am until closing daily. Brunch: 11
am–3 pm Saturday, Sunday. Cards: V. FITCH, FOX &
BROWN, Telephone: (202) 289-1100. Brunch: 11 am–
3 pm Saturday, Sunday. Lunch: 11:30 am–5 pm Monday–
Friday; 11 am–5 pm Saturday. Dinner: 5 pm–10 pm
Sunday–Thursday; 5 pm–11 pm Friday, Saturday.
Cards: AE, CB, DC, MC, V. RICHARD'S and FET-
TUCCINE'S, Telephone: (202) 789-0394. Hours:
11:30–11 pm daily. Cards: AE, CB, DC, MC, V. All
restaurants: Reservations suggested. Street parking or
nearby parking lot. Full bar service. Wheelchair access.

Washington: Downtown
PICCOLO MONDO
Italian

$$

The look of this basement Italian restaurant is pure New York. The below-ground location is turned to advantage with a Fred Astaire-style Art Deco stairway and chrome and etched glass, which are the decorative antipasto to this multiroom dining enclave. Next is a bar fashioned of pastel lights and fans of silvery metal strips. Then the dining rooms, so divided and reflected in mirrors that you can feel both private and within an endless labyrinth of diners. But don't let the decorative style of the restaurant influence your ordering; the simplest dishes are best. A homely dish like pasta and bean soup is extremely good. Fried mozzarella celebrates simplicity— just cheese and bread, perfectly fried. Cold red peppers contrast well with unctuous eggplant and acid capers. And zucchini rises above its cliches with an airy veal stuffing or fried in the lightest of batters. Pastas are as delicate as one would wish, and in most cases their sauces are boldly seasoned. As for main courses, fish and veal show this kitchen to advantage, and the zesty tomato sauces are the kitchen's highlights. Despite the restaurant's flashy style, the best of its food is the down-to-earth, hearty and bold southern Italian cooking.

PICCOLO MONDO, 1835 K Street NW, Washington. Telephone: (202) 223-6661. Lunch: noon–2:30 pm Monday–Friday. Dinner: 6 pm–11 pm Monday–Friday, 6–11 pm Saturday. Closed Sunday. Cards: AE, CB, DC, MC, V. Reservations required. Street parking. Full bar service. Non-smoking area.

PETITTO'S
Italian $$

The accumulation of details adds up to a pleasant evening at Petitto's, enough to make you overlook its shortcomings. First, the two small rooms are stylish, one with a fireplace, the other with a picture window overlooking a bit of greenery. The walls are hung with amusing pen-and-ink drawings on a pasta theme. The wine list is small but reasonable, and the house wines are commendable. Dinner is served by young people who seem like professionals in training rather than between-job chorines. The menu is devoted almost entirely to pastas, though some of the best dishes—veal sauteed with lime and butter, leg of lamb roasted with rosemary and garlic—are meat specials. The antipasto is a beautiful still life. As for pastas, the noodles are slightly too thick, and the tomato sauces are more notable than the cream sauces, but in general the food has a fresh liveliness. Pasta prices are high, but orders are available in half portions.

PETITTO'S, 2653 Connecticut Avenue NW, Washington. Telephone: (202) 667-5350. Lunch: 11:30 am–2:30 pm Monday–Friday. Dinner: 6 pm–10:30 pm Monday–Saturday. Closed Sunday. Cards: AE, CB, DC, MC, V. Reservations suggested. Street parking or nearby lot. Full bar service. Jacket recommended.

Dinner

Antipasti

*Antipasto, 5.75

Prosciutto & Frutte, 5.25
(fresh fruit of the season with prosciutto)

*Vongole Alla Marinara 5.00
(whole clams sautéed in olive oil and herbs)

Zuppa del Giorno
(soup of the day)

Insalate

Insalata Verde, 2.75
(tossed green salad)

Insalata Mista, 3.75
(romaine, tomatoes, mushrooms and parmesan)

*Insalata Caprese, (in season) 4.75
(tomatoes, mushrooms, basil and our own mozzarella)

Specialita

Pane Petitto	Bruschetta	Panzanella
(fried bread) ●	(bread toasted with garlic, parmesan, oil and salt)	(bread toasted with tomatoes, parmesan and basil)
2.00	1.50	2.00

Entrees

Fettuccine:
(Our Own Egg Noodles)

*Falasche Alla Petitto, 8.25
(cream, mushrooms, prosciutto and peas)

All' Alfredo Di Roma, 7.75
(with cream, butter and parmesan)

Falasche Alla Bolognese, 7.75
(spinach noodles with veal and tomato sauce)

Con Basilico & Pomodoro, 7.50
(with basil and tomato sauce)

Salsa Di Carne
(Sauces with Meat)

*Penne Con Salsiccia & Funghi, 8.00
(sliced Italian sausage, mushrooms, fresh tomatoes, red wine and garlic)

Lasagna Alla Petitto, 7.75
(tomato and bechamel sauce, veal, mozzarella and parmesan cheese, mushrooms and our own egg noodles)

Tortellini Con Crema Al Pomodoro, 8.00
(spinach and white pasta filled with meat and served with cream or tomato sauce)

*Penne Alla Matriciana, 7.75
(with bacon, tomato sauce, hot peppers and Romano cheese)

* House Specialty
A Charge of 5.00 will be added when only one entree is served for two people,
or when no entree is ordered.

115

Washington: Downtown
PRIME RIB
Steakhouse

$$$

Bear in mind that the Prime Rib is a specialty restaurant; when you forget that, your dinner is in trouble. It is Washington's most glamorous setting for plain old steak and roast beef, with gold-bordered black walls and a pianist playing a very grand piano. The beef is fine: roast beef is thick and tender, though not always rare or juicy; steak is crusty and as rare as ordered. Shredded fresh horseradish on the side is a thoughtful touch. And crab is high quality here. But none of the above can withstand the brusque, indifferent service and the insipid and overpriced appetizers. Venture, if you will, into crisped potato skins for a side dish and creamy cheesecake for dessert. And investigate the in-depth list of American red wines. But beef and gilt are what warrant the Prime Rib's hefty prices.

PRIME RIB, 2020 K Street NW, Washington. Telephone: (202) 466-8811. Lunch: 11:30 am–3 pm Monday–Friday. Dinner: 5 pm–11 pm Monday–Saturday. Closed Sunday. Cards: AE, CB, DC, MC, V. Reservations suggested. Free valet parking. Full bar service. Wheelchair access. Jacket and tie required.

Washington: Downtown
ROOF TERRACE
American

$$

Born with a silver spoon in its mouth, this glorious-looking dining room is wasting its inheritance. It has its proximity to the city's concert and theater halls. It has a grandly high ceiling dripping with crystal chandeliers and window walls overlooking Washington. And it has service so indifferent that it can take over an hour to get a cup of coffee at brunch (and then coffee bitter enough that one could wish for tea). Good ideas are there: late supper or brunch of poached eggs with Smithfield ham on a biscuit with hollandaise. I have found a few successes, among them a sorbet of kiwi and banana that is a delightful combination. But more frequently the food shows the effects of feeding the masses—in incompetent reheating, indifferent seasoning, the kind of nobody's-in-charge tone. The room is magnificent, the menu clever. But the Roof Terrace food and service show a restaurant catering to a captive audience.

ROOF TERRACE, 2700 F Street NW (in the Kennedy Center), Washington. Telephone: (202) 833-8870. Brunch: 11:30 am–3 pm Sunday. Lunch: 11:30 am–3 pm Monday–Saturday. Dinner: 5:30 pm–8 pm Monday–Friday. Supper: 9:30 pm–half hour after last curtain Friday, Saturday. Cards: AE, CB, DC, MC, V. Reservations recommended. Garage parking. Full bar service. Wheelchair access. Non-smoking area.

Washington: Georgetown
1789
French

$$$

On one block of 36th Street in Georgetown are three restaurants that serve three different purposes, each of them well. F. Scott's is Washington's supreme supper club; The Tombs serves a good collegiate snack. And then there is 1789, a pretty and serene 18th-century house serving up-to-date and imaginative French food. The dining rooms are charming, painted in colonial gɩeige, with fireplaces and nicely detailed furnishings, from the candle holders to the etchings of early Washington. The menu is long—two dozen appetizers, main dishes from rabbit to reindeer. But most interesting are the daily specials: oysters in puff pastry or in garlic-parsley butter (plump Wellfleet oysters, just warmed rather than overcooked); salmon sauced with two caviars or stuffed with spinach; pheasant or lamb, or sweetbreads in orange sauce—all on one day. The cooking shows character and ability. Sauces are delicate, vegetables are beautifully cooked and sensitively seasoned. Chicken breast with pecans and morels is not a knockout, but it is a well-prepared and utterly pleasant dish. Grilled lobster was slightly undercooked on one occasion, but it was as fresh as one could hope and accompanied with a dill-caviar sauce that suited it well. Standards are high. One could wish for a more informative or evenly and modestly priced wine list, but the choices are intriguing. And for dessert, 1789 serves such extravaganzas as gateau St.-Honore under a cloud of spun sugar.

1789, 1226 36th Street NW, Washington. Telephone: (202) 965-1789. Dinner: 6 pm–11 pm Monday–Thursday; 6 pm–midnight Friday, Saturday. Closed Sunday. Cards: AE, CB, DC, MC, V. Reservations required. Valet parking. Full bar service. Wheelchair access. Jacket and tie required.

ENTRÉES

LES POISSONS ET CRUSTACÉS

SOLE DE DOUVRES SAUTÉE MEUNIÈRE
Dover Sole in Lemon Butter $17.95

CREVETTES CORSINI
Shrimp Sauteed in Garlic $18.50

OU CHABLIS
Or Sauteed in White Wine $18.00

AIGUILLETTE DE ROUGET DE ROCHE À L'ESTRAGON
Red Snapper with Tarragon and Dill $17.00

ESPADON GRILLÉ LYONNAISE
Broiled Swordfish with Sauteed Onions $16.50

SAUMON POCHÉ ROUGE ET NOIRE
Poached Salmon with Red and Black Caviar $18.50

FILETS DE SOLE FARCIS À LA MOUSSE DE SAUMON
Stuffed Filet of Sole with Salmon Mousse $19.00

FILET DE STRIPED BASS À LA MOUTARDE DE MEAUX
Filet of Striped Bass with Mustard Seed $17.00

ÉMINCÉ DE QUEUES DE HOMARD ET CREVETTES AU CITRON VERT
Lobster Tail and Shrimp in Lime $21.00

RAGOÛT DE HOMARD ÉCORCÉ AVEC JULIENNE
Shelled Lobster in Cream   (Prix du Jour)

HOMARD DU MAINE GRILLÉ
Broiled Lobster   (Prix du Jour)

LES ENTRÉES VOLANTES

FOIE DE VEAU À L'ANGLAISE OU PROVENÇALE
Calves Liver with Bacon or Garlic Butter $16.25

RIS DE VEAU AVEC ORANGE ET POIVRE VERT
Sweetbreads with Orange and Green Peppercorn $16.50

CANARD RÔTI À L'ORANGE OU CASSIS
Roast Duck with Orange or Black Currant $16.50

MAGRET DE CANARD AUX COEURS D'ARTICHAUX
Sauteed Breast of Duck with Artichoke Hearts and Mushrooms $18.50

CAILLES FARCIES AU FOIE DE CANARD ET RIS DE VEAU
Stuffed Quail with Duck Liver and Sweetbreads $19.00

FAISAN AU VINAIGRE DE POIRE À LA MOUSSE DE MARRONS
Pheasant with Pear Vinegar, Chestnut Mousse $18.75

SUPRÊME DE POULET AUX POIREAUX
Chicken Breast with Leeks and Basil $16.25

Washington: Downtown
SHEZAN ✱
Indian $$

Shezan is a jewel box lined with deep-wine colors and trimmed with glowing brass. This Pakistani restaurant can introduce you to the subtlety and complexity of the food of the Indian subcontinent even if you don't like hot spices. The food is mild, but rarely dull. Visit Shezan for its tandoori chicken. Permeated with the smoke imparted by a tandoori clay oven, its skin russet and crisp, its meat juicy and tingling with spices, this chicken is a good value. Lamb kebab is excellent, its meat marinated and crusty, still rare inside. Even the grilled shrimp is golden from its marinade and full of intricate seasoning. But fish has been the greatest disappointment. It was chewy, dry and tasted more of fish than any fish should, with a sauce much too thick. Concentrate on grilled entrees and consider vegetable side dishes—chick-peas with tamarind and coriander, spinach with potatoes, or vegetable kebabs—to fill out your meal.

SHEZAN, 913 19th Street NW, Washington. Telephone: (202) 659-5555. Lunch: noon–3 pm Monday–Friday. Dinner: 6 pm–11 pm Monday–Saturday. Closed Sunday. Cards: AE, CB, DC, MC, V. Reservations suggested. Free garage parking. Full bar service. Wheelchair access.

MURGH TIKKA LAHORI   8.50

Spring chicken lightly marinated in spices
and lemon juice, barbecued over flaming
charcoal in the Tandoor.

SHEESH KEBAB SULTANI   10.25

Tender morsels of lamb marinated in our
special recipe, watched over by Ali Baba's
genie, broiled with complimenting
additions on the grill.

SHEESH KEBAB MURGH   8.75

"Don't leave me off the skewer" said the
chick; so we didn't. It's scrumptious—
marinated pieces of chicken, broiled on
the grill.

SHEESH KEBAB KABULI   10.25

Preferred by the tribesmen of the North-
western Frontier Province—diced sirloin
of beef, mildly marinated, broiled on
skewers with tomatoes, onions and bell
peppers.

KARAHI KEBAB KHYBERI   8.75

A specialty from the Khyber Pass region:
diced chicken grilled with Hymalayan
herbs, tomatoes and capsicum in the traditional iron "Karahi"—brought sizzling to
your table.

SEEKH KEBAB MUGHLAI   8.25

Ground sirloin of beef blended with herbs
and spice, left to marinate then broiled on
skewers over charcoal in the Tandoor—a
delicious "nibble" with drinks, or, as a part
of the feast.

Washington: Downtown
SHOLL'S CAFETERIA ✳
American

$

One of Washington's finest features is the Sholl's Cafeteria duet, and even more so since the Connecticut Avenue branch was moved to K Street in bright expanded surroundings. The tearoomy furnishings were preserved, and even the bag ladies made the move. Still the food remains—with a few exceptions—as fresh and satisfying and inexpensive as ever. At rock-bottom prices you don't expect veal cutlet to be more than a breaded vealburger, and cafeteria fried fish is bound to be overexposed to heat. Nevertheless, they are pleasant foods, accompanied with fresh vegetables, freshly made salads such as potato and cucumber, homemade biscuits, cornbread and doughnuts, ripe melons and other fruits, fine custards and puddings and famous pies—though the last sample of apple pie tasted of canned apples. Foods are cooked in small quantities to avoid steam-table fatigue. The quality and freshness of the foodstuffs are stunning at the price.

SHOLL'S CAFETERIA, 1990 K Street NW, Washington. Telephone: (202) 296-3065. Breakfast: 7 am–10:30 am Monday–Saturday. Lunch: 11 am–2:30 pm Monday–Saturday. Dinner: 4 pm–8 pm Monday–Saturday. Closed Sunday. No credit cards. No reservations. Street parking. No alcoholic beverages.

Washington: Georgetown
SUSHI-KO
Japanese

$ $

This, Washington's first sushi restaurant, has heavy competition these days, but still holds its own in the sushi department. Its tiny dining rooms pack more tables than ever, and some of its delicate beauty is thus disrupted, but it still rings true in its Japanese style. Its finest moment is lunch, when the menu is severely limited—just very good sushi and sashimi, interesting dumplings heavy on the garlic, ginger and hot pepper but very light on the noodle wrapper, teriyaki, a couple of soups, and tempura that may run heavy and gummy and is best not chanced. But most delightful of all, is a compartmented lacquer bento box arranged with a charming collection of edibles: sushi rice wrapped in seaweed and marching across one compartment, and in the others a few bites of pristine raw tuna in a garden of multicolored curly leaves, a few squares of sweet-savory chicken and grilled fish, marinated vegetables cut into flowers and geometric shapes or wrapped into gift-worthy packages, and slivers of pickled ginger and cabbage. It is plentiful and as festive as having your gifts and eating them, too.

SUSHI-KO, 2309 Wisconsin Avenue NW, Washington. Telephone: (202) 333-4187. Lunch: noon–2:30 pm Tuesday–Friday. Dinner: 5 pm–10:30 pm Tuesday–Saturday; 5 pm–10 pm Sunday. Closed Monday. Cards: AE, V. Reservations suggested. Parking lot. Full bar service. Wheelchair access.

Washington: Downtown
SPECTRUM
American $

This charming minimalist sculpture of an eating place would be at home in SoHo or overlooking San Francisco Bay, but it's actually one block from the Washington Convention Center. And it's a perfect advertisement for the Washington restaurant renaissance, offering imaginatively prepared seafood, chicken and veal dishes, many of them Mexican in inspiration, reasonable prices and comfortable, colorful surroundings. The best value I encountered was a veal francaise at lunch, five scallops of high-quality veal sauteed with butter, lemon and parsley and served over fettuccine that soaked up the delicious pan juices. The Italian house wine is good, the coffee excellent.

SPECTRUM, 919 11th Street NW, Washington. Telephone: (202) 638-7505. Lunch: 11 am–3 pm Monday–Friday. Dinner: 5 pm–11 pm Monday–Saturday. Closed Sunday. Cards: AE, CB, DC, MC, V. Reservations suggested. Street parking or nearby lot. Full bar service.

APPETIZERS

CEVICHE $5.70
A FRESH FLOUNDER & SCALLOP MARINADE SERVED WITH AVOCADO & ONION IN LEMON SHELLS.

GUACAMOLE $4.75
MADE TO ORDER. THIS BLEND OF AVOCADO, TOMATO, ONION, LEMON & CORIANDER, SERVED WITH HOMEMADE TORTILLA CHIPS

GAMBAS AL AJILLO $5.25
SAUTÉED TENDER SHIRMP IN GARLIC SAUCE SERVED WITH TOAST POINTS.

CALAMARI FRITTI $4.25
A MOUND OF TENDER FRIED SQUID WITH VERY LIGHT LEMON SAUCE.

BAKED STUFFED CLAMS $4.50
HOMEMADE. THIS TENDER DELIGHT OF FRESH CHOPPED CLAMS IN WINE, GARLIC, BREAD CRUMBS, PARSLEY & LEMON

SOUPS

CREAM OF BLACK BEAN $2.50
THIS SECRET RECIPE IS THE CREAM OF THE CROP TOPPED WITH CHOPPED GREEN ONION & CILANTRO

SOUP DU JOUR $2.50

SALADS

CAESAR SALAD $4.75
A SKILLFUL BLEND OF ROMAINE, CROUTONS PARMIGIAN, ANCHOVIES, EGG, GARLIC, OLIVE OIL, BLACK PEPPER & VINEGAR

ROQUEFORT SALAD $5.50
ROMAINE LETTUCE SERVED WITH A VINAIGRETTE DRESSING & TOPPED WITH ROQUEFORT CHEESE.

HOUSE SALAD SMALL $1.75 LARGE $3.00

ENTRÉES

CHICKEN ENCHILADAS $9.95
TENDER PIECES OF CHICKEN, WRAPPED IN OUR HOMEMADE TORTILLA, SERVED WITH ENCHILADA SAUCE & SOUR CREAM

CHICKEN IN TRADITIONAL MEXICAN MOLE $9.95
SAUTÉED BREAST OF CHICKEN IN AN EXOTIC SAUCE, WITH RICE, REFRIED BEANS & WARM TORTILLAS

CHICKEN PRINCESS $9.95
MOIST CHICKEN BREAST IN CREAM SAUCE WITH MUSHROOMS, SERVED WITH RICE & VEGETABLES

CHEESE ENCHILADAS $8.50
OUR TORTILLAS POACHED IN ENCHILADA SAUCE, WRAPPED AROUND JACK CHEESE & BAKED WITH ENCHILADA SAUCE
SERVED WITH RICE & BEANS

VEAL FRANÇAISE $9.95
SAUTÉED MEDALLIONS OF VEAL DIPPED IN EGG BATTER. SAUCE OF GLEE. BUTTER, LEMON, WINE & PARSLEY

VEAL MARSALA $9.95
MEDALLIONS OF VEAL SAUTÉED WITH MARSALA WINE & MUSHROOMS SERVED WITH VEGETABLES

RAINBOW TROUT $10.95
STUFFED WITH SHRIMP, HEARTS OF PALM & MUSHROOMS SERVED WITH VEGETABLES

FILET OF FLOUNDER $8.95
SAUTÉED IN BUTTER, WHITE WINE & PARSLEY, SERVED WITH VEGETABLES

NEW YORK STRIP STEAK $10.95
EIGHT OUNCE CENTER CUT SAUTÉED WITH CRUSHED BLACK PEPPER, GLEE, BRANDY & MUSHROOMS

SCALLOPS IN SAFFRON $9.95
TENDER BAY SCALLOPS SAUTÉED WITH MUSHROOMS, TOMATO, CREAM, BRANDY & SAFFRON SERVED OVER RICE

MUSSELS AU VIN $8.75
STEAMED MUSSELS WITH ONION, WINE, PARSLEY, BROTH & HERBS SERVED WITH RICE

MUSSELS MARINARA $8.75
STEAMED MUSSELS WITH TOMATOES & SERVED OVER FETTUCCINE

HOMEMADE DESSERTS

CHEESE CAKE $2.50   CRÈME CARAMEL $2.50
DESSERT DU JOUR $2.50   SORBET WITH RASPBERRY SAUCE $2.50

ALL FOODS SERVED HERE ARE PREPARED AT THE TIME OF YOUR ORDER & MAY REQUIRE A SHORT WAIT
WE HOPE YOU WILL ENJOY DINING WITH US

SUZANNE'S
American $\$\$$

Suzanne's is like a neighbor's house where you stop for a drink and stay for dinner. Up a narrow staircase and as noisy as a house party, Suzanne's attraction is sociability rather than comfort. Don't expect a serene and smoothly served lunch and dinner. Do expect bright, fresh and creative food that sometimes works and sometimes falls a little flat. And a chance to venture into some excellent (and naturally, pricey) wines by the glass. Suzanne's is the casual kind of cafe where *she* might have just a piece of cake (the chocolate chestnut cake if she's smart) and *he* might have a cheese platter, where *he* might have just a bowl of soup and *she* might have a whole poached baby salmon. The best bets are the cold plates, perhaps with the most succulent of smoked chicken or beef fillet with a herbed mayonnaise. Chicken salad is likely to be wonderful, and whatever is fashionable—cold pasta with pesto, snow peas with red peppers—can be seen, tasted and, more often than not, enjoyed. Then if you like it, you can buy more to take home from the "carry out" downstairs.

SUZANNE'S, 1735 Connecticut Avenue NW, Washington. Telephone: (202) 483-4633. Lunch: 11:30 am–2:30 pm Monday–Friday; 11:30 am–3 pm Saturday. Dinner: 6 pm–10:30 pm Monday–Thursday; 6 pm–11:30 pm Friday, Saturday. Closed Sunday. Cards: MC, V. No reservations. Street parking. Full bar service.

20 March 85

SUZANNE'S

wine bar & restaurant/upstairs

Wednesday Dinner Menu

Minestrone vegetable soup w/ risotto + ham 3⁰⁰

Salmon + Nori Mousse 3⁷⁵

Walnut + Spinach Pâté 3⁷⁵

Pâté Maison 3⁴⁵

Arugula, Watercress, + Belgian Endive Salad 3⁹⁵

Rainbow Trout stuffed w/ asparagus, pimentos + leeks, w/ Parsley Sauce 13⁹⁵

Salmon Steak w/ Cepe Sauce 12⁹⁵

Pork Loin w/ Brandied Fruit Butter 11⁹⁵

Cornish Game Hen w/ Morel Sauce 11⁹⁵

Lamb Medallions w/ Chevre + Sun Dried Tomato Sauce 12²⁵

Cold Loin of Veal w/ Spinach Sauce 12⁹⁵

Duck Breast w/ Banana Sauce 13⁹⁵

Asparagus Strudel 10⁴⁵

Filet Mignon w/ Green Peppercorn Butter 11⁹⁵

HOURS
Lunch: 11:30 - 2:30 Mon. - Fri.
('til 3:00 on Sat.)
Dinner: 6:00 - 10:30 Mon. - Thurs.
('til 11:30 on Fri. & Sat.)
Wine, Spirits & Desserts: 11:30 am - 11:00 pm Mon. - Thurs.
('til 1:00 am on Fri. & Sat.)

*daily specials*wines by the glass*cheese platters*pate platters*great homemade desserts*

Washington: Downtown
SZECHUAN ✳
Chinese

$$

By now Szechuanese restaurants have been around long enough that they can be called old fashioned, and that's what this one is—old fashioned, good, reliable. The menu is extensive, and the cooking plays with fire but also offers the interplay of flavors that makes the fire worthwhile. There are flaws—pasty spring roll fillings, crumbly dumpling wrappers, hot-and-sour soup that needs to be more of both. And hot brown sauces tend to have a sameness. But there are plenty of redeeming features in the fresh and lightly cooked seafoods; whole fish Szechuan style, teasing with its balance of sweetness and hotness; stir-fried asparagus; the complex and delicate flavors and textures of orange beef. Szechuan has been redecorated—it is now Mediterranean blue with acres of mirrors—and the staff has been spruced up to serve graciously and swiftly.

SZECHUAN, 615 I Street NW, Washington. Telephone: (202) 393-0130. Hours: 11 am–11 pm Monday–Thursday; 11 am–12 pm Friday, Saturday; 11 am–10 pm Sunday. Cards: AE, V. Reservations suggested for parties of four or more. Street parking or nearby parking lot. Full bar service.

川湘名菜

鼓汁雞傑 * CHICKEN with BLACK BEAN SAUCE 9.45

湖南雞傑 * CHICKEN, Hunan Style 9.45

宮保雞片 * CHICKEN with WINE SAUCE 9.45

湖南鴨片 * SLICED DUCK, Hunan Style 9.95

四川鴨具 * SHREDDED DUCK, Szechuan Style 9.95

鼓椒鴨片 * SLICED DUCK in BLACK BEAN SAUCE 9.95

魚香鴨片 * SLICED DUCK in GARLIC SAUCE 9.95

湖南羊肉 * LAMB, Hunan Style 9.45

四川羊肉 * LAMB, Szechuan Style 9.45

魚香羊肉 * LAMB, with CHEF'S GARLIC SAUCE 9.45

湖南牛柳 * STEAK, Hunan Style 9.45

鐵板牛柳 * SIZZLING STEAK 11.95

香脆魚脯 CRISPY FISH CHUNKS, CHEF'S SPECIAL 8.95

鼓汁蒸魚 STEAMED FISH with BLACK BEAN SAUCE 11.95

豆瓣魚 * HOUSE SPECIAL FISH, Szechuan Style 11.95

香脆全魚 * HOUSE SPECIAL CRISPY WHOLE FISH 11.95

酒釀魚卷 * HOUSE SPECIAL FISH ROLL with RICE WINE 11.95

花菜蝦丸 SHRIMP BALL with CAULIFLOWER 10.45

四川蝦丸 * SZECHUAN SHRIMP BALL, CHEF'S SAUCE 10.45

洞庭蝦先 TUNG TING SHRIMP 10.45

長沙蝦片 SLICED SHRIMP CHANG-SHA SPECIAL 10.45

油爆蝦片 JUMBO SHRIMP with CHEF'S CUT CHOICE VEGETABLES 10.45

紅燒蝦球 * JUMBO SHRIMP with BROWN SAUCE 10.45

湖南蝦片 * SHRIMP, Hunan Style 10.45

牛柳蝦丸 * SHRIMP BALL with BEEF & VEGETABLES 10.95

炒 三 鮮 TRIPLE DELIGHT with CHINESE VEGETABLES

         & CHEF'S SAUCE (Chicken, Pork & Shrimp) 10.95

湖南干貝 * SCALLOPS, Hunan Style 10.45

炒 雙 鮮 SCALLOPS and SHRIMP with VEGETABLES 10.95

魚香雙鮮 * SCALLOPS and SHRIMP with GARLIC SAUCE 10.95

鼓椒雙鮮 * SCALLOPS and SHRIMP with BLACK BEAN SAUCE 11.95

中式干貝 * SCALLOPS with WINE SAUCE 11.95

海鮮雀巢 SEAFOOD COMBINATON in THE BIRD NEST 13.95

什錦雀巢 * MIXED DELIGHT in THE BIRD NEST 13.95

TABARD INN
American $$

Tabard Inn still comes off as an able amateur, full of
clever ideas and good taste, a little awkward in the
execution. Any sunny lunchtime, though, you will have
to wait for either the garden or the indoor dining room,
which is colorful and as clattery as a college student
union. The food is inventive—American, generally good,
sometimes astonishingly pretty. The emphasis is on
seasonal, fresh fish and vegetables, plus home-style
desserts that are likely knockouts. The moderate prices
and the friendly bustle compensate when the chicken
salad has blundered into three ingredients too many or
the waiter has brought your entree while you're still
eating soup.

TABARD INN, 1739 N Street NW, Washington. Tele-
phone: (202) 785-1277. Breakfast: 7 am–10:30 am
Monday–Friday; 8 am–10:30 am Saturday, Sunday.
Lunch: 11:30 am–2:45 pm Monday–Friday. Dinner: 6
pm–10:30 pm Monday–Wednesday; 6 pm–11 pm Thurs-
day–Saturday; 6 pm–10 pm Sunday. Cards: MC, V.
Reservations suggested. Street parking or nearby lot.
Full bar service. Wheelchair access.

Appetizers & Salads

Cassolette
of Brie & Almonds
4.50

Gravlax
Cured Norwegian Salmon
with crème fraîche mustard sauce
4.75

Pâté or Terrine Maison
priced daily

Caesar Salad
Romaine lettuce with toasted French bread
croutons & Parmesan cheese
3.75

Tabard Salad of the Evening
4.00

Entrees

Garnett Chopped Steak
with Maitre d'Hôtel butter
10.25

Sauteed Breast of Chicken
stuffed with apples, Jarlsberg cheese
& cider sauce
12.25

Glazed Duck Breast
grilled & served with Tabard chutney
12.75

Oven Braised Salmon
with horseradish-mustard
cream sauce
12.50

131

What once showed promise as Washington's most exceptional sushi bar has come up short this year, slipping in the quality of its fish and the imaginativeness of its offerings. What the menu calls its top grade assortment is a pedestrian array no different from other sushi bars' regulars, and the fish has lacked its former pristine firm texture and clean taste. An interesting possibility for lunch is a pretty bento box of cooked seafood, but while its fried shrimp and scallops have been delectably light and crisp-coated, the assortment is mostly rice and pickles, plus a quadrant of iceberg lettuce and pale tomatoes; it adds up to spare rations.

TAKESUSHI, 1010 20th Street NW, Washington. Telephone: (202) 466-3798. Lunch: noon–2:30 pm Monday–Friday. Dinner: 5:30 pm–10 pm Monday–Friday; 5 pm–10 pm Saturday. Closed Sunday. Cards: AE, CB, DC, MC, V. Reservations suggested. Street parking. Full bar service.

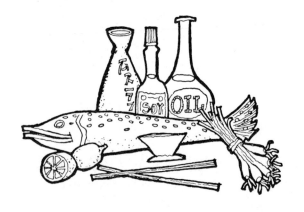

Washington: Georgetown
TANDOOR
Indian

$$

Indian restaurants are expected to be either bare-bones neutral or ornate. Tandoor is a visual surprise, its small dining rooms bright with orange lacquered chairs and cloths of contemporary design. Nobody would blink if it were Scandinavian. The focal point is obviously Indian, the tandoor oven behind a glass wall, where the chef skewers chicken, lamb and seafood and suspends them in the oven to cook. It is a magnetic show and properly tempts you to order from the tandoor-oven specialties. Start with a beer or a Pimm's cup, a faintly sweet alcoholic drink stirred with a cucumber stick. With it have an assortment of appetizers, the best of which are grilled ground-lamb kebabs called kofta. Skip the tandoori platter that mixes the grilled meats and seafoods. Chicken dishes are the best preparations, red-tinged from their yogurt and spice marinade, smoky but mildly seasoned. The menu also lists many curries and the range of Indian dishes, but sometimes they are very good, other times disappointing. Accompany your meal with tandoor-cooked bread; obviously, the tandoor oven gets the chef's greatest attention. The waiter may suggest side dishes, but keep in mind that they rapidly elevate the bill. Desserts, if you like intensely sweet Indian desserts, are well made here, and you can end with milky tea spiced with fennel and cardamom.

TANDOOR, 3316 M Street NW, Washington. Telephone: (202) 333-3376. Lunch: 11:30 am–2:30 pm daily. Dinner: 5:30 pm–11 pm daily. Cards: AE, CB, DC, MC, V. Reservations suggested. Parking in commercial lot in rear. Full bar service. Wheelchair access. Non-smoking area.

TAVERNA THE GREEK ISLANDS
Middle Eastern (Greek)　　　　　　　**$**

The old reliable A & K Restaurant has spread out and changed its name; in fact, it has changed a lot, with remarkably little effect on the food (which was always good) and the prices (which were always low). Besides the usual kebabs, moussaka and lamb stews, a culinary focal point is exohico, a lamb pie wrapped in buttery phyllo and stuffed with juicy lamb cubes, green olives, artichoke hearts and cheese. Accompany it with a choice of several Greek wines, which are sold by the glass as well as by the bottle.

TAVERNA THE GREEK ISLANDS, 307 Pennsylvania Avenue SE, Washington. Telephone: (202) 547-8360. Hours: 11 am–11:30 pm Monday–Saturday; 4 pm–10 pm Sunday. Cards: AE, CB, DC, V. No reservations for lunch except for large groups of ten or more, accepted for dinner. Street parking. Full bar service. Nonsmoking area.

HOUSE SPECIALTIES

LIGO APO OLA – assortment of greek specialties, mousaka, pastichio, dolmades, souzoukakia, lamb, spanakopita and more. 17.95

MOUSAKA ALLA GREEK ISLANDS – layers of ground beef and eggplant, wine flavored, topped with besamela sauce. 7.50

KOTOPOULO PSITO PATATES FOURNOU – Grecian style ½ chicken and potatoes, oven baked in butter, lemon, garlic sauce. 7.95

AMBELOFILODOLMADES – grape leaves stuffed with ground beef, rice and herbs, cooked with egg and lemon sauce. 8.95

SOUZOUKAKIA PIKANTIKA – meatballs flavored with cumin, wine tomato sauce and herbs, served with rice. ... 6.95

PASTICHIO ITHAKA STYLE – layers of freshly ground beef and macaroni, herbs, wine flavored, topped with besamela sauce. 7.50

LAGOS KRASATOS – rabbit cooked in Greek wine, tomatoes, and herbs, served with rice. 7.95

MELITZANES IMAM BAYLDE – meatless, stuffed eggplant with herbs, garlic, onions, parsley and tomatoes, served with oven potato and Greek cheese. 6.95

MOSHARI
BEEF

MOSHARI STEFADO – chunks of beef braised and simmered in a tomato, wine and vinegar sauce with baby onions, served and baked in a casserole. Served with rice. 7.95

ARNI
LAMB

ARNI KAPAMA MOREA STYLE – chunks of lamb cooked with fresh mushrooms in greek wine kapama sauce, served with rice 7.95

ARNI YOUVECHI IERA PETRA STYLE – chunks of lamb and orizo cooked with tomatoes, romano cheese, and herbs, baked in casserole.. 7.95

ARNI AGINARES AVGOLEMONO – lamb and artichokes cooked in egg and lemon sauce, served with rice.. 7.95

THALASINA
SEAFOOD

PSARI SKARAS – fresh whole fish in season basted with lemon, garlic and olive oil ....

GARIDES TIGANITES – fried jumbo shrimp. 9.95

FILETTO GLOSSA TIGANITI – fried fillet of fish. 8.95

KAVOUROKEFTEDES – fried crab cakes. 9.95

The Above Thalasina Served with Fried Potatoes.

135

THAI TASTE
Thai $

Art Deco Americana never looked better. Thai Taste is a charming dining room, matched and even bettered by the service. As in most Thai restaurants, appetizers are priced only slightly lower than main dishes. That is appropriate, as the appetizers are very large portions and the main dishes tend to be smallish. Don't short-change the appetizers—concentrate on them. It is hard to pass up the satay and the fried stuffed chicken wings. Nor would I miss charcoal-grilled chicken if it is among the specials; in fact, I might order it as a main course instead. There are cold, peppery and lemony salads of minced cooked meats or seafoods. There are fried spring rolls and won tons, and there is a delicious and unusual fried salted beef. The soups can be outstanding. But main dishes are more variable in quality, indeed, less exciting. From the standing menu try Thai beef, or chicken with cashews. But focus on daily specials, particularly the seasonal ones such as oysters or char-broiled whole crabs. Each day brings a different steamed fish, with lemon grass or ginger and "salt prunes," or with pork, mushrooms and bamboo shoots. In many dishes, particularly main courses, Thai Taste mutes its pepperiness, so if you like your food searing, ask them to turn up the heat. If you don't like hot food, ask questions, since the meat salads and soups can be inflammatory. Thai Taste has taken an old tradition—Arbaugh's rib restaurant, a Washington landmark—and restored its dining room to offer delicate and intricate Thai cooking and exceptionally gracious service at a very low price.

THAI TASTE, 2606 Connecticut Avenue NW, Washington. Telephone: (202) 387-8876. Hours: 11:30 am–10 pm Monday–Thursday; 11:30 am–10:30 pm Friday, Saturday; 5 pm–10 pm Sunday. Cards: AE, DC, MC, V. Reservations suggested. Street parking. Full bar service.

อาหารทะเล

SEA FOOD

GOONG OHB MOR DIN กุ้งอบหม้อดิน   8.25
Shrimp cooked in a pot with herbs.

GOONG OHB LAO DANG กุ้งอบเหล้าแดง   8.25
Shrimp cooked in wine sauce.

GOONG PAHD NRMAI FA-RAHNG กุ้งผัดหน่อไม้ฝรั่ง   8.25
Shrimp with asparagus.
                                              (Seasonal)

GOONG PAHD YORD PUCK กุ้งผัดยอดผัก   8.25
Shrimp with Chinese vegetables.

LOOGCHIN GOONG PAHD PUCK SOPON ลูกชิ้นกุ้งผัดผัก   6.25
Shrimp balls with green cabbage.

GOONG PUD PED กุ้งผัดเผ็ด   8.25
Shrimp sauteed in red curry.

GOONG PUD PRIK PAO กุ้งผัดพริกเผา   8.25
Shrimp sauteed with chili and spring onion.

POO NIM PUD PRIK PAO ปูนิ่มผัดพริกเผา   8.95
Soft shell crab sauteed with chili.

ปูนิ่มผัดผงกะหรี่
POO NIM PUD PONG CURRY   8.95
Soft shell crab sauteed with curry powder and spring onion.

Washington: Downtown
TIBERIO
Italian

$$$

Elegant but not inspired is this northern Italian restaurant that competes with the French for top expense accounts. The large dining room is filled with roses and decorated in a contemporary simplicity one equates with unadorned diamond pendants. Waiters in black-tie serve in a manner that veers from well oiled to oily, depending on their workload and your status. The food is reliable but rarely wonderful, though its prices suggest something more. True, Tiberio sets high standards for itself: it has raspberries year round, and fresh asparagus more likely than not. But it goes in for routine elegance rather than surprises. The fish may be nicely cooked, but topped with nothing more thrilling than tasteless frozen baby shrimp, commendable asparagus and lemon butter. Unlike Vincenzo, Tiberio doesn't offer adventures like fresh sardines or razor clams. Surprisingly, therefore,

PESCE
fish

TROTA ALLA SAVOIARDA   21.95
fresh trout with onions, mushrooms and spicy breadcrumbs

FRITTO MISTO MARE   22.95
crisply fried baby calamari, sole, scallops and baby marrows

SCAMPI CAPRESE   23.95
scampi cooked with mushrooms, garlic, tomato and white wine

FILETTI DI SOGLIOLA PAESTUM   23.95
poached filets of dover sole with white wine sauce, sliced tomato, oysters

SOGLIOLA DI DOVER ARLECCHINO   23.95
dover sole in white wine with artichoke, mushrooms and baby shrimp

SOGLIOLA DI DOVER AL LIMONE   23.95
dover sole sauteed in butter with lemon

ARAGOSTA ALLA GRIGLIO   31.00
large fresh Maine lobster broiled, served with melted butter

ARAGOSTA FRA DIAVOLO   31.00
large fresh Maine lobster broiled with a piquant tomato sauce

ARAGOSTA CAPRESE   31.00
large fresh Maine lobster baked with garlic, butter and bread crumbs

Tiberio can do its best with earthy dishes: the best dish in my recent memory was a robust lentil soup. The menu concentrates on fish and veal, but the veal is likely to be overpounded and lacking succulence, though it is meat of high quality. While Tiberio has the most expensive pasta dish in town and an astonishing tariff for its typical pastas at dinner, it still makes fine spinach-stuffed agnolotti in a dense cream sauce. You can wash them down with perhaps the most overpriced wines in an American restaurant, and follow with desserts that are beautiful, fairly good but similarly overpriced. In other words, Tiberio is a reasonably good restaurant with an inflated sense of its own worth.

TIBERIO, 1915 K Street NW, Washington. Telephone: (202) 452-1915. Lunch: noon–3 pm Monday–Friday. Dinner: 6 pm–11 pm Monday–Saturday. Closed Sunday. Cards: AE, CB, DC, MC, V. Reservations suggested. Valet parking or nearby lot. Full bar service. Wheelchair access. Jacket and tie required.

CARNI
entrees

PETTO DI POLLO 'VILLA JOVIS'   21.95
deep fried rolled chicken breast filled with parsley and garlic butter

SOVRANA DI POLLO ALLA VESUVIANA   21.95
chicken breast, tomato ragu, fried eggplant and mozzarella

NODINO DI VITELLO AI CARBONI VIVI   23.95
veal cutlet cooked simply on the grill

SCALOPPA DI VITELLO ALLA 'MINORESE'   21.95
veal escalope cooked with fresh peppers, oregano, tomato and a touch of garlic

SCALOPPINE DI VITELLO SORRENTINA   22.95
veal scallopini sauteed with prosciutto and mozzarella chees

PICCATA AL LIMONE   21.95
veal scaloppini with butter and lemon

PICCATINE DI VITELLO 'AMERIGO VESPUCCI'   22.95
a veal dish of scaloppine, brandy, mushrooms and creamy truffled wine sauce

COSTOLETTA DI VITELLO ALLA DUCALE   23.95
veal cutlet sauteed, garnished with mushrooms and fresh artichoke

FRACOSTA DI MANZO PALERMITANA   23.95
sauteed sirloin steak served with sweet peppers, oregano, mushrooms and olives

139

Washington: Georgetown
TOUT VA BIEN
French

$$

In Georgetown, one usually has the choice of good food, moderate prices, attractive environment, solicitous service or a compelling menu. But rarely more than one or two at a time. Tout Va Bien allows you to choose all of the above, with only a little compromising here and there. The culinary interest centers on the list of daily specials. Among them, liver is a particular favorite, and no wonder; it is delicate and tender meat, not only perfectly sauteed, but topped with slices of avocado that suit it well and sauced with shallots and herbs and a light wash of brown sauce. Delightful dish. Several fish are regularly on the menu, but with something new about them each time. Or one could have skewered lamb, chicken with five kinds of peppers, or pork loin. Appetizers have individuality; the prettiest dish you'll find in any modest French restaurant being the spinach pate offered here, a rectangle of dark green, banded with white fat and centered with a pale, rosy chicken liver and cubes of pink ham. It tends to be overseasoned with nutmeg, but maintains a freshness and lightness. Desserts are given even greater care. Several tarts are listed each day, their asset being their last-minute assembly of fresh fruit or berries with a light custard on a base of still-crisp puff pastry. Fresh ideas, details that compensate for flaws, food that is above the routine but not complicated and moderate prices all add up at Tout Va Bien not to a brilliant star among restaurants, but to a nice place to eat. A city never has too many of them.

TOUT VA BIEN, 1063 31st Street NW, Washington. Telephone: (202) 965-1212. Lunch: 11:30 am–2:30 pm Monday–Saturday. Dinner: 5:30 pm–11 pm Monday–Saturday; 5:30 pm–10:30 pm Sunday. Cards: AE, MC, V. Reservations suggested. Nearby parking lot. Full bar service.

Washington: Downtown & Capitol Hill
TIMBERLAKE'S
American $

Generally you go to a neighborhood pub for neighborliness, and at Timberlake's you get plenty of that. The room is full of materials—brick, wood—that exude warmth, the bar is long and well attended, and the place is as noisy as it should be, considering that it is a pub. But the food is even better than it should be. Appetizers run from oysters to very good fried cheese sticks, and you could hardly do better than hanging around Timberlake's with a beer and a couple of appetizers. Dinner entrees are more variable, while the sandwiches have maintained their reputation. Salads are big and beautiful. Quiches are soft and fresh custards filled with delicacies like lobster and mushrooms—good productions. For a drinking place, Timberlake's has good eating. And now it has an offspring on Capitol Hill.

TIMBERLAKE'S Downtown location: 1726 Connecticut Avenue NW, Washington. Telephone: (202) 483-2266. Capitol Hill location: 231 Pennsylvania Avenue SE, Washington. Telephone: (202) 543-8337. Hours: 11:30 am–2 pm Monday–Thursday; 11:30 am–3 pm Friday; 10:30 am–3 pm Saturday; 10:30 am–2 pm Sunday. Cards: AE, CB, DC, MC, V. No reservations. Street parking. Full bar service. Wheelchair access.

Washington: Capitol Hill
209-1/2 ✳
American

$ $ $

This classic of new American cuisine still holds its own. The small dining room remains delicately pretty, and the small menu which changes each season still comes up with new and irresistible choices. In summer the softshell crabs are the sweetest to be had, getting along surprisingly well with garlic, ginger and herbes de provence. Meats are given more-than-typical attention, as in grilling marinated pork chops and then anointing them with watercress butter. Cold platters are picturesque and designed as well for taste as for appearance. Start with some new-to-Washington aperitif, continue to an herbed vegetable or pasta appetizer (don't miss the ratatouille when it is available), and, if you are indecisive, choose a main dish that includes the best dish in the house, zucchini fritters. Small and lovely, with a continuing air of invention, freshness and charm in the environment as well as the food, 209-1/2 is a place to display for people who scoff at American cooking. And it remains Capitol Hill's best restaurant.

209-1/2, 209-1/2 Pennsylvania Avenue SE, Washington. Telephone: (202) 544-6352. Lunch: 11:30 am–2:30 pm Monday–Friday. Dinner: 6 pm–10:30 pm Monday–Thursday; 6 pm–11:30 pm Friday, Saturday. Closed Sunday. Cards: AE, CB, DC, MC, V. Reservations suggested. Street parking. Full bar service.

*dinner may be ordered à la carte or as a
prix fixe dinner including appetizer, entrée
and choice of dessert*

appetizers   3.95

pasta with walnut-ricotta sauce
"green" minestrone with tortellini
cold eggplant lasagna
   with seasoned oil and vinegar
hot spicy shrimp over
   cold marinated spaghettini   *(supp. 7.00)*
arugula, watercress, and romaine
   with gorgonzola oil
leeks and buffalo mozzarella

à la
carte

Red Snapper Tonnato   16.95
a sauce of cold tuna and herbs is dressed over red snapper,
served with vinegar-pickled zucchini and penne

Calf's Liver Veneziana   14.95
calf's liver is served with a pancetta onion marmalade
presented with zucchini pancakes

Maharajah Veal Milanese.   15.95
scallopini of veal is fried with a hint of curry, served with
zucchini pancakes, hollandaise sauce and pear chutney

The Intrigue Steak   17.95
a fillet is served with a porcini sauce, presented with zucchini
pancakes and fresh artichoke

Muscovy Duck with Vinegar Sauce   17.95
breast of muscovy duck is served rare with a sauce of vinegar
and shallots and zucchini pancakes

The Theatre Supper   *prix fixe*
a three course dinner changing nightly, served before
7:00 pm and after 9:30 pm

intriguing desserts   3.95

fresh pears with gorgonzola butter
italian bread pudding with marsala
sour cream chocolate cake
cheesecake in a snifter with warm caramel sauce

VAL DE LOIRE
French   **$$**

This is no gastronomic palace, but it is a nice little French restaurant, the kind that in many American cities would be a standout. Val de Loire is comfortable, a good value in a useful location. Half the menu is seafoods, and Val de Loire does them credit. Side dishes show much concern: nicely browned potatoes, firm and buttery green beans, unctuous ratatouille. Val de Loire is a creditable if not glorious restaurant with traditional French cooking, its sauces flour thickened and its vegetables served as side dishes rather than precious gems to garnish a plate. Paris is full of them, but 15th Street is obviously happy to have it.

VAL DE LOIRE, 915 15th Street NW, Washington, Telephone: (202) 737-4445. Lunch: 11:30 am–2:30 pm Monday–Friday. Dinner: 5:30 pm–10:30 pm Monday–Saturday. Closed Sunday. Cards: AE, CB, DC, MC, V. Reservations required. Parking lot. Full bar service. Wheelchair access. Jacket and tie required.

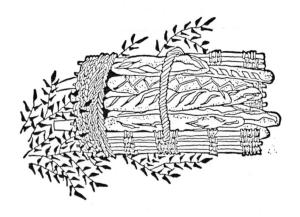

Washington: Downtown
VINCENZO ✳
Italian

$$$

When people ask for a good seafood restaurant they aren't usually thinking Italian, but they should be; Vincenzo is top-notch as a seafood restaurant and is one of the very best Italian restaurants as well. How does it do it? Simply. Impeccably fresh fish, marinated in olive oil and grilled, or sauteed with white wine or braised with vegetables. Or maybe a mixture of briny-fresh seafoods fried in the lightest of batters and oils or stewed with tomatoes. To start, there is a rolling cart of marinated vegetables and fish salads as antipasti (be sure to try the eggplant). Then there are a few pastas such as linguine with a sprightly touch of tomato, herbs and crab or perhaps linguine with clams, garlic and parsley. A couple of nearly bare whitewashed rooms with tile floor, sensational chewy country bread with a crust that is nearly indestructible, a good Italian wine list and a group of waiters who by now know their food and their customers well—all add up to a mature, reliable and delicious restaurant.

VINCENZO, 1606 20th Street NW, Washington. Telephone: (202) 667-0047. Lunch: noon–2 pm Monday–Friday. Dinner: 6 pm–10 pm Monday–Saturday. Closed Sunday. Cards: AE, MC, V. Reservations suggested. Street parking or nearby parking lot. Full bar service.

WASHINGTON PALM
Steakhouse   **$$$**

It doesn't have the sawdust on the floor like the New
York Palm, and the beef has not quite the same
character, but this Washington branch of that famous
steakhouse has definite rewards. The steak is reliable if
not glorious; it is thick and crusty and rare when you ask.
It can be served a la Palm with onions and red peppers,
sliced and bedded on toast to absorb the juices—
sometimes chewy but very good. If you can't decide
between the hash browns or the Palm fries, try half of
each. They are grand, as are the vegetables when they
are not overcooked. Lobsters are giant, but one could
cost a family's weekly food budget. At lunch, don't pass
up the soup—one of the best in town, and at a startling
low price. Part of the Palm's trademark is the service, a
routine of camaraderie and fraternity jokes, fun if not
always efficient.

WASHINGTON PALM, 1225 19th Street NW, Wash-
ington. Telephone: (202) 293-9091. Hours: 11:45 am–
10 pm Monday–Friday; 6 pm–10:30 pm Saturday.
Closed Sunday. Cards: AE, CB, DC, MC, V. Reservations
required. Free valet parking for dinner. Full bar service.
Wheelchair access.

Appetizers

Shrimp Cocktail	7.50	Snow Crab Claws	7.50
Crabmeat Cocktail	8.50	Clams on the Half Shell	5.50
Melon & Prosciutto	6.00	Clams Casino	7.00
Oysters Rockefeller	7.50	Oysters on the Half Shell	5.50
Smoked Mussels	7.00	Smoked Trout	7.00

Soup du Jour   2.25

Onion Soup Gratinee   2.75

Palm's Hot Garlic Bread   1.50

Entrés

PRIME AGED N.Y. Sirloin Steak	21.00
Steak a la Palm	23.00
Filet Mignon	21.00
Prime Ribs of Beef	17.50
3 Double Rib Lamb Chops	18.50
PRIME AGED N.Y. Double Sirloin Steak	42.00
JUMBO LOBSTERS	According to Size
Roast Long Island Duck	13.00
Chicken Oregenato	12.00
Linguini, with Red or White Clam Sauce	10.00
Veal Picata	16.00
Veal Parmigiana	16.00
Fresh Fish of the Day	——

New American cooking is leaping forward among restaurant trends, but it has run a slow pace in Washington. Want to know what it is? Try West End Cafe. Its two rooms are attractive, the service staff performs smoothly, and the menu changes seasonally. What's even better, the food is inventive without being quirky and is prepared with skill. Furthermore, the choices and the tastes are far from routine. Start with grilled, fresh shiitake mushrooms with garlic butter—or whatever wild mushrooms are in season. Or sample smoked salmon minced into a creamy and tangy tartare. Main dishes include modernized coq au vin, grilled meats with special touches such as basil and a faintly sweet glaze on lamb chops. Fish is fresh and treated with respect. There is also a list of light fare—eggs Benedict, chili, unusual sandwiches and salads. Desserts include homey and delicious apples baked in buttery phyllo or a cheesecake—perhaps Mexican style. West End Cafe is evolving into one of the brightest of Washington's easygoing but sophisticated small restaurants.

WEST END CAFE, One Washington Circle NW, Washington. Telephone: (202) 293-5390. Breakfast: 7 am–10 am Monday–Friday; 8 am–10:30 am Saturday, Sunday. Brunch: 11:30 am–3 pm Saturday, Sunday. Lunch: 11:30 am–2:30 pm Monday–Friday. Dinner: 6 pm–11:30 pm Monday–Thursday; 6 pm–midnight Friday, Saturday; 6 pm–1 am Sunday. Cards: AE, CB, DC, MC, V. Reservations suggested. Street parking or nearby lot. Full bar service. Wheelchair access.

SPLENDID FARE

Spicy Shrimp Brochettes 13.25
served with tufts of boston lettuce, a selection of thinly sliced cucumbers
radishes & scallions and gently steamed brown rice

Fish of the Day (market price)

Barbecued Sesame Duck 9.95

Duck with Raspberry Sauce 9.95

Glazed Game Hen Chinatown 10.25
accompanied by brown rice, braised red cabbage and apples
and a honey mustard sauce

Fennelled Chicken 9.75
served on a bed of brown rice with sautéed spinach & garlic

Calf's Liver 9.15
with mustard-watercress sauce

Giant Grilled Veal Chop 16.25
a 12-oz. veal chop finished with a fresh herb-mustard butter
and accompanied by roasted red peppers & lacy potato pancakes (dinner only)

Basil-broiled Lamb Chops 13.35
accompanied by white beans bretonne

Filet Steak Bearnaise 12.65
served with vegetable brochettes

LIGHT FARE

A Salmon Sampler 11.95
salmon three ways – gravlaks, scottish smoked & smoked salmon tartare
served with fresh asparagus and a variety of accompaniments

Salade Gourmande 12.10
a selection of radicchio, boston, romaine, snowpeas & enoki mushrooms,
lightly tossed in a vinaigrette, accompanied by three jumbo shrimp
and a wedge of triple-creme cheese

Duffy's London Broil Salad 8.40
a greek-style salad served with rare london broil

Italian Salami Sandwich 7.95
layers of genoa salami, soppresata, smoked mozzarella, watercress
and an olive mustard butter on a crusty whole wheat bread,
accompanied by a melange of fresh fruit

The Ultimate Curried Chicken Salad 7.95
served in a papaya with appropriate accompaniments

Breast of Chicken Club Sandwich a la Harry's Bar 6.25
our traditionally delicious sandwich comprised of fresh chicken,
crisp bacon, lettuce, tomato, and a fried egg (lunch only)

Hamburger or Cheeseburger on French Bread 6.10
with french fries or onion rings

Eggs Benedict 6.10

The Grand Chili Bowl 6.25
served with sour cream, cheddar cheese and green peppers

WINTERGARDEN AND TERRACE RESTAURANTS
Continental

$$

The Watergate's Terrace has been steadily pulling ahead of the crowd into top quality. Always good, solid and dependable, it is now an excellent choice for pre-theater dining and an outstanding place for Sunday brunch. Fish is served proudly here—very fresh fish, cooked to retain velvety, juicy texture, sauced with something that enhances rather than drowns, perhaps a fine bercy sauce. The menu balances the standards—steak, roast beef, rack of lamb—with some original twists, particularly in veal dishes. Dessert, as in the old days, is still Watergate pastries, but this grand restaurant has seen the light otherwise. If you are looking for space, comfort, smooth and elegant service with good food near the Kennedy Center, the Terrace now fills that bill.

WINTERGARDEN AND TERRACE RESTAURANTS, 2650 Virginia Avenue NW, Washington. Telephone: (202) 298-4455. Breakfast: 7 am–10 am Monday–Saturday; 7 am–11 am Sunday. Brunch: 11:30 am–2:30 pm Sunday. Lunch: 11:30 am–2:30 pm Monday–Saturday. Dinner: 5 pm–midnight Monday–Saturday; 5 pm–11 pm Sunday. Cards: AE, CB, DC, MC, V. Reservations suggested. Valet parking. Full bar service. Wheelchair access.

FISH & SHELLFISH

Grilled Salmon Steak with Tarragon Butter   _18.00_

Dover Sole Meunière   _18.25_

Red Snapper Braised with Vermouth and Vegetables   _18.50_

Sauteed Jumbo Shrimp Herb Saint with Linguine Pesto   _18.75_

Rainbow Trout with Toasted Pinenuts   _14.50_

Broiled Sea Scallops Norfolk Style in Duchesse Potatoes   _17.50_

Broiled Lobster Tail with Drawn Butter   _29.75_

Baked Crab Imperial   _18.00_

MEAT & POULTRY

Tenderloin of Veal with Morel Sauce, Fettuccine Alfredo   _19.75_

"Weinerschnitzel" Escalope of Veal Viennese Style   _17.00_

Scaloppine of Turkey Breast and Asparagus, Glazed
with Muenster Cheese   _16.00_

Dry Aged Prime Rib, Horseradish Cream   _18.00_

Dry Aged Prime N.Y. Sirloin Steak _(12 oz.)_   _24.00_

Filet Mignon "Rossini," Foie Gras and Truffles   _21.50_

Chateaubriand, Sauce Bearnaise, Bouquetière of Vegetables   _44.00_

Double Cut Lamb Chops   _19.00_

Roast Rack of Lamb, Bouquetière of Vegetables _(for two)_   _44.00_

Sauteed Breast of Chicken, Cream of Peppercorn and Armagnac _15.00_

Roast Breast of Duck with Sweet Dark Cherries,
Walnuts & Kirsch   _16.00_

YOSAKU
Japanese $$\$\$$

Even with sushi bars opening in nearly every neighbor-hood, Yosaku stands out as a good value and for its special offerings. As for the value, the sushi assortment costs $10.50 and includes eight pieces of sushi and one tuna roll, which seems an average count among local sushi bars. Another facet of value, though, is that you can order single pieces of sushi a la carte, where most Japanese restaurants sell them only in pairs. Thus, for a not outlandish price, you can put together your own assortment with all your favorites. The sushi here are just fine, the fish sufficiently fresh and the rice well made. The chef will concoct special requests, though sometimes items on the sushi menu are not available. Certainly a sushi fan will want to try the appetizer specials such as partially cooked tuna in vinegar, raw fish with a delicious sweet-salty miso sauce, sometimes raw fresh abalone. There is also a full Japanese menu in this small, reasonably attractive dining room, and upstairs is a Japanese lounge and nightclub. Good service, modest prices, good food—Yosaku is the neigh-borhood restaurant of a sushi lover's dreams.

YOSAKU, 4712 Wisconsin Avenue NW, Washington. Telephone: (202) 363-4453. Lunch: noon–2:30 pm Monday–Friday. Dinner: 5:30 pm–midnight Monday–Sunday. Cards: AE, MC, V. No reservations. Street parking. Full bar service.

MARYLAND

Maryland: Chevy Chase
AMERICAN CAFE
American   **$$**

See review in Washington section page 3.

AMERICAN CAFE, 5252 Wisconsin Avenue, Chevy Chase, Maryland. Telephone: (301) 363-5400. Hours: 11 am–2 am Monday–Thursday; 11 am–3 am Friday, Saturday; 10:30 am–2 am Sunday. Cards: AE, CB, DC, MC, V. Reservations suggested for large parties. Nearby parking lot. Full bar service. Wheelchair access.

Maryland: Silver Spring
ARIRANG HOUSE RESTAURANT
Korean   **$**

Arirang is a Korean restaurant with a fifteen-page menu ranging from Korean to Chinese to Japanese dishes and translated only randomly. The waitresses not only speak English haltingly but may understand it even less. No matter, with many of the dishes only $5 to $6, with portions very large and with almost all of the food at least tasty and some spectacularly savory, it is worth taking a few chances. The dining room is as casual as they come. And no matter what you order your table will be crowded with little dishes, for kim chee, marinated vegetables and a tea tasting like liquid Rice Krispies simply appear. Be sure to order one of the first dishes on the menu, barbecued meats, whether thinly sliced beef (bul go ki), short ribs or pork. Also try the thick starchy and spicy pancakes, studded with scallions or fish or a mixture of meat and vegetables. Then there is bibim bob, a delicious production number of raw or cooked beef to toss at the table with spinach, bean sprouts, soy nuts, tree ears, fried egg, red pepper paste and fat, chewy rice—in all it puts fried rice to shame. Or you could fill up on a giant bowl of soup, perhaps with slices

154

of radishes, garlic, scallions and peppers, along with transparent noodles and short ribs. The rest of the menu sinks into mysteries—intestines and vegetables or buckwheat noodles topped with various things. There are sushi and Chinese dishes, too. But keep in mind that the staff is Korean, so order accordingly.

ARIRANG, 7918 Georgia Avenue, Silver Spring, Maryland. Telephone: (301) 587-4501. Hours: 11 am–10:30 pm daily. Cards: AE, MC, V. Reservations suggested. Nearby parking lot. Full bar service.

아리랑 특별메뉴

Arirang Special Menu

A-1 순 대 (1접시)	Soon Dae *(Korean sausage)*		$ 7.95
A-2 빈 대 떡	Bindae Deuk *(Korean style green bean Pancake)*		$ 3.95
A-3 파 전	Pa Jeon *(Korean style green onion pancake)*		$ 5.95
A-4 생 선 전	Saengsun Jeon *(Korean style fish pancake)*		$ 7.95
A-5 순 대 국	Soondae Guk *(soup with Korean sausage)*		$ 5.95
A-6 홍 어 회	Hongoe Hoe *(sliced raw stake with hot sauce)*		$ 8.50
A-7 계 장 백 반	Gaejang Baek Ban *(steamed rice with seasoning crab)*		$ 6.25

* 주문 대 환영

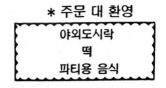

야외도시락
떡
파티용 음식

Maryland: Chevy Chase
CHINA CORAL ✻
Chinese

$$

Some of Washington's best seafood restaurants are also its best ethnic restaurants, and one of the tops on the Chinese list is China Coral. Lively trout and lobsters in tanks near the entrance bode well, as does the menu's list of crabs, conch, eels, snails, abalone, shrimp, scallops, oysters, clams and fin fish prepared in ways more varied than usual. Focus on the fresh fish—steamed, boiled, deep-fried or stir-fried—and on complex dishes such as fish rolls stuffed with ham or crepes rolled with shrimp paste. Order seafoods in softshell crabs, blue crabs and the like. This is a big and bustling restaurant, where service is thoughtful when the evening is quiet but erratic at crowded times. Dim sum, also seafood oriented, are available at lunch, and the list of meat dishes is as long as any nonseafood restaurant.

CHINA CORAL, 6900 Wisconsin Avenue, Chevy Chase, Maryland. Telephone: (301) 656-1203. Hours: 11:30 am–10:30 pm Monday–Thursday; 11:30 am–11:30 pm Friday; 11 am–11:30 pm Saturday; 11 am–10 pm Sunday. Cards: AE, CB, DC, MC, V. Reservations suggested. Parking lot. Full bar service. Wheelchair access.

★ SZECHUAN FISHROLL **8.95**
Fresh fillet of fish rolled and filled with shredded ham, bamboo shoots, and spring onions. Lightly battered and deep fried until golden brown. Topped with chef's special Szechuan sauce.

CHINA CORAL BIRD'S NEST **13.95**
Lobster, king crabmeat, shrimp, and scallops sauteed with baby corn, fresh snowpeas, mushroom, and carrots served in a delicious nest of crispy potato.

★ SAUTEED STUFFED SCALLOPS **8.95**
Fresh scallops stuffed with minced shrimp and sauteed in spicy black bean sauce.

CORAL DRAGON and PHOENIX COMBINATION **8.95**
Jumbo crystal shrimp and tender fillet of chicken sauteed with snowpeas, bamboo shoots, mushroom, and carrot flowers.

SIZZLING FIVE FLAVOR VOLCANO SHRIMP **10.95**
Jumbo shrimp in shell to retain delicious flavor. Served on a sizzling iron platter with onions and topped with chef's special sauce and flaming cognac.

SIZZLING FISH STEAKS **11.95**
Fresh fish steak with onions in chef's special sauce. Served on a sizzling iron platter.

SIZZLING SEAFOOD COMBINATION **13.95**
Treasures of the sea: lobster, shrimp, scallops and king crabmeat sauteed with fresh vegetables. Served on a sizzling iron platter.

CHINA CORAL SHRIMP CREPES **8.95**
Delicious minced shrimp filled delicate egg crepes. Deep fried until golden brown, sliced and served with special sauce.

CRISPY STUFFED DUCKLING **10.95**
Boneless duck stuffed with minced shrimp. Deep fried and served with chef's special sauce.

★ ORANGE FLAVOR BEEF **9.95**
Tenderloin beef, sauteed in a spicy orange flavor sauce.

GIANT SQUID in BROWN SAUCE **10.95**
Fresh giant squid, carved into tender flowery pieces, quickly sauteed in chef's special brown sauce with water chestnuts and straw mushrooms.

SAI SEE LOBSTER KEW **14.95**
Lobster meat sauteed in creamy egg-white sauce served over crispy bean thread noodles. A special name for this delicate dish for a special you!

CRISPY FLOUNDER KEW **14.95**
Fresh whole flounder is filleted and sauteed with selected vegetables. Served on the flounder frame that's deep fried to a crispy golden brown.

★ SPICY MONGOLIAN LAMB **9.45**
Tender slices of lamb sauteed in famous spicy ginger & scallion sauce.

STEAMED WHOLE SEA BASS **11.95**
Fresh whole sea bass steamed with ginger, black bean sauce and special seasonings.

★ SHRIMP BALLS and BEEF **8.95**
Shrimp balls and tender beef sauteed with vegetables in a hot spicy sauce.

PHOENIX BIRD'S NEST **8.95**
Marinated boneless chicken chunks sauteed with plum sauce and served in a delicious bird's nest of crispy potato.

KINGDOM SPARERIBS CANTONESE STYLE **8.95**
Center cut pork loin chunks, marinated and sauteed in our special sauce. It's finger licking delicious!

★ CURRIED SHREDDED BEEF **8.95**
Shredded beef, onions, carrots and asparagus all in chef's special curried sauce.

Maryland: Silver Spring
CRISFIELD ✳
Seafood

$$

Washingtonians will put up with anything for good seafood. They will wait in line. They will crowd into small ugly booths. They will pay high prices and not mind having their silverware handed to them in a bundle and their plates slid across the table to them. In fact, they love the hassle, at least at Crisfield. Outsiders might not understand what's so special. After all, the clam chowder tastes halfway between New York and Boston, the menu lists frozen lobster tails as the only lobster dishes, and bleu cheese with crackers sells as a dessert. But ignore the seafoods imported from any farther than the Chesapeake Bay. Eat oysters or clams on the half shell, stewed or steamed. Concentrate on crab meat and broiled fish. The imperial crab, or even better the flounder or rockfish stuffed with crab, or even the buttery crab Norfolk will leave you dreaming fondly of the line in front of Crisfield. Don't bother with elaborations like shrimp Creole and, if you need dessert, Gifford's ice cream is just down the road. Frying is a high art at Crisfield, from the softshell crabs to the french fries. You might have guessed from the beginning that any restaurant this ugly and this crowded has to be good.

CRISFIELD, 8012 Georgia Avenue, Silver Spring, Maryland. Telephone: (301) 589-1306. Hours: 11 am–10 pm Tuesday–Thursday; 11 am–10:30 pm Friday, Saturday; noon–9 pm Sunday. Closed Monday. No credit cards. No reservations. Street parking. Beer and wine only.

Maryland: Bethesda
KABUL WEST ✳
Middle Eastern

$

In the past few years Afghan restaurants have flourished in the Washington area. Kabul West is an especially endearing one. The dimly lit brick-walled room has just enough greenery and homeland photographs to make dinner feel special. And the food is reliable Afghan cooking, which means delicious. Start with aushak, homemade noodles stuffed with scallions and topped with tomato-meat sauce, yogurt and mint. The same topping enhances eggplant and squash, and the noodle melange also comes as a soup, aush. Main courses are browned rice mixtures with meat and sweet accents of raisins and glazed carrot. Kebabs are exceedingly tender and well perfumed from their marinades, cooked just right and in generous servings. For dessert, try a platter-size fried wisp of dough topped with sugar and chopped pistachios. This is food of delicacy and modest prices.

KABUL WEST, 4871 Cordell Avenue, Bethesda, Maryland. Telephone: (301) 986-8566. Lunch: 11:30 am–2 pm Monday–Friday. Dinner: 5:30 pm–10 pm Sunday–Thursday; 5:30 pm–11 pm Friday, Saturday. Cards: MC, V. Reservations suggested. Street parking or nearby lot. Beer and wine only. Wheelchair access.

Maryland: Bethesda
LA MICHE
French   **$$**

Rough, pale wooden beams turn Bethesda office archi-
tecture into a vision of a farmhouse, with baskets hung
from every rafter. On some walls are flowered cafe
curtains, on others bucolic wallpaper. Waitresses' accents
are French, their delivery smooth and expert. Appetizers
are adventurous, starting with oysters poached with
orange butter. Brioche and croissants are used as
containers for wine-sauced chicken livers and scallops.
The duck, confit de canard, is deliciously browned in its
own fat. Grilled lobster has been perfectly timed and
sauced with a soft cloud of white butter sauce. Well-
prepared vegetables garnish the plates. To finish,
besides very reasonably priced and creditable souffles,
there is tarte tatin that is quite good. In all, a meal at La
Miche is a treat, except for occasional lapses.

LA MICHE, 7905 Norfolk Avenue, Bethesda, Maryland.
Telephone: (301) 986-0707. Lunch: 11:30 am–2:30 pm
Monday–Friday. Dinner: 6 pm–10 pm Monday–Saturday.
Closed Sunday. Cards: MC, V. Reservations accepted
for dinner. Valet parking. Full bar service. Wheelchair
access.

Maryland: Hyattsville
LEDO
Italian $

Practically a historical monument in Prince George's County, Ledo signals that it is open by the lines of people waiting to get in. They crowd the booths set with paper place mats. They order pizza and more pizza, flaky-crusted and thickly sealed with tomato sauce and cheese. The food is not grand, but it is tasty home-grown fare, the house tomato sauce a kind of trademark, thick and too sweet, but zesty. Some dishes—for example, veal "ala Francea"—are eccentric but nevertheless endearing. Don't look for elegant food here. Skip the shrimp. For inexpensive, solid food Ledo packs them in.

LEDO, 2420 University Boulevard East, Hyattsville, Maryland. Telephone: (301) 422-8122. Hours: 8 am–midnight Sunday–Thursday; 8 am–1 am Friday–Saturday. Cards: MC, V. No reservations. Nearby parking lot. Full bar service. Wheelchair access. Non-smoking area.

Maryland: Bethesda
LA PANETTERIA
Italian

$

Pizza, crunchy-crusted homebaked bread and focaccia, a spongy garlic-spiked flat bread, are the stars at La Panetteria. And the setting adds up to one of the most attractive pizza parlors to be seen, an indoor courtyard with tile floor and whitewashed walls, decorated with half roofs which nearly convince you that you are outdoors. The tables are heavy wood and left bare. In all, it conjures up a sunny day in the Italian countryside. Think picnic and you will dine well at La Panetteria. Salads of perfect simplicity, some uncomplicated seafoods, perhaps pasta. The more elegant dishes are more variable. Keep in mind that the name refers to bread baking. Stray if you must, but hone in on the pizza and focaccia.

LA PANETTERIA, 4921 Cordell Avenue, Bethesda, Maryland. Telephone: (301) 951-6433. Lunch: 11:30 am–3 pm Monday–Friday. Early Bird Dining: 4 pm–6:30 pm Monday–Friday. Dinner: 4 pm–10 pm Monday–Sunday. Cards: AE, MC, V. Reservations suggested. Nearby parking lot. Beer and wine only. Wheelchair access.

SALSICCE AND PEPPERONI VERDE ALA POMODORO **7.95**
*Our Fennel Flavored Sausage sauteed with Fresh Onion, Mushroom
and Green Peppers, Marinara Salsa and a side of Linguine*

LASAGNA ALLA FORNO **7.25**
*Curled pasta noodles, fresh ricotta cheese, Ground Veal and Beef, Tomato Salsa,
Parmesan and Provolone Cheese baked together in a casserole*

FETTUCINE *Freshly prepared; to order, your choice* **8.45**
Alla Pano, Carbonara, Funghi alla Crema, Marinara Parmesan

THE ITALIAN COMBINATION **9.45**
*A sampler of La Panetteria's finest and freshest, Cannoli, Tortteline,
Sausage, Meatball, Spaghetti and Mussels*

EGGPLANT PARMGIANA **6.95**
Style thin slice layers of egg plant topped with provolone cheese

CARNE

VEAL MARSALA **8.95**
Escallops of Veal Fresh Mushrooms in a piquant Marsala Salsa

VEAL PARMIGIANA **8.75**
Scallops of veal sauteed in marinara salsa topped with provolone cheese

VEAL GERMANIA **8.45**
Cutlet of Veal Capers and Anchovy

VEAL FRANCESCA **8.45**
Cutlet of Veal, Lemon Wedge

BISTECCA ALA PIZZIOLA **9.95**
Delmonico Steak Sauteed with Garlic. Onion and Green Peppers

POLLO

PICCATA **8.25**
*Tender scallops of chicken breast sauteed in a piquant caper
lemon butter sauce*

CASINO **7.95**
Village style Chicken Breast Potpurri of Vegetables baked casserole

CHICKEN ARTICHOKE **8.95**
Baked Chicken in Marinara Salsa, Artichokes, Green Peppers and Black Olives

PESCE

FRUTTI DI MARE **9.95**
Mussel, Clam, Lagousta, Fish assorted served on a bed of Linguine

PESCATORE DELLA JOURNA **9.95**
*Absolutely Fresh Filet of the Day Broiled with herbs and served on
sliced Egg Plant*

COZZE ALLA MARINARA **6.95**
*Fresh mussles sauteed in oil, garlic, wine and spicy marinara sauce,
served with linguine*

VONGOLE ALLA MARINARA **6.95**
Fresh clams, sauteed in oil, garlic, parsley, tomatoe, served with spaghetti

SARDELLE FRITTE **6.95**
Fried smelts, served with a spicy vinegrette sauce and lemon

CALAMARI ALLA LUCIANA **6.95**
*Squid sauteed with oil, garlic, parsley and spicy marinara sauce,
served with linguine*

CALAMARI FRITTI **7.95**
Crisply fried calamari squid, served with nothing, no, no, with a lemon

*Above served with spaghetti, insalata, bread and made here in our kitchen.
We offer a variety of fresh pasta.*

Maryland: Bethesda
LE MARMITON
French

$$

What makes Le Marmiton special is, foremost, its menu, which is printed daily and ranges through a dozen appetizers, a few soups, salads and nearly a dozen and a half main dishes. Cream of crab soup with almonds, radish leaf soup, brioche toast of chanterelles and marrow, fettuccine in cream sauce with smoked duck and oregano. Those are just appetizers. Main dishes have been exceptionally good. One night sweetbreads were breaded in fresh crumbs and sauteed perfectly, nicely sparked by a sauce of lemon and fresh basil. Lamb has been sauteed and teamed with julienned ginger in a sauce of mild but lingering flavor. Veal is beautifully prepared, neither cut too thin nor pounded too hard nor cooked too long, served with a simple earthy topping of shiitake and oyster mushrooms. There are tropical star fruit or quinces to serve with duck, fresh herbs to season meats, and fresh monkfish, tuna and dover sole in the fish section. A main dish might come with six vegetables, and they taste as good as they look. The pastry chef keeps busy at Le Marmiton, and finally there is good coffee, particularly good decaffeinated espresso. So here is some uncommonly charming French food, and the prices—moderate to high—justifiably reflect it. Finally, the room is attractive in a quiet provencal mood, with flowered wallpaper and sheer lacy curtains.

LE MARMITON, 4931 Cordell Avenue, Bethesda, Maryland. Telephone: (301) 986-5188. Lunch: 11:30 am–2:30 pm Monday–Friday. Dinner: 6 pm–10 pm Monday–Thursday; 6 pm–10:30 pm Friday, Saturday. Closed Sunday. Cards: AE, CB, DC, MC, V. Reservations suggested. Street parking or nearby lot. Full bar service. Wheelchair access.

Le Marmiton
March 12, 1985
BONSOUR, ET BON APPETIT!!

Appetizers

Country Pâté with Green Pepper Corns	$3.75
Artichoke Vinaigrette	4.50
Green Asparagus Vinaigrette	5.00
Baked Mussels with Butter & Garlic	5.50
Toast of Brioche with Wild Mushrooms & Marrow	5.75
Escargot in Potato Skins	6.00
Shrimp & Sea Scallops in Salmon & Scallop Mousse	6.00
Ceviché of Rockfish, Salmon & Bay Scallops	6.50
Gravlax of Norwegian Salmon	6.50
Long Island Oysters, on the Half Shell with Basil Vinegar or Baked with Buerre Blanc & Mint	6.50

Soupes

Watercress Soup	3.25
Cream of Crab with Almond	4.00
Lobster Consommé aux Petits Legumes & Bay Scallops	4.25

Salades

Caesar Salad	4.25
Belgian Endive with Raddichio, Apple & Pistachio	4.00
Endive, Raddichio & Watercress	4.25
Mache with Goat Cheese	4.50

Viandes

Calf Brain Sautéed with Capers	$ 11.00
Lamb Medaillon with Ginger	13.50
Lamb Tournedos with Mint & Brown Sauce	14.50
Sweetbreads, Breaded, with Cream Sauce	15.00
Breast of Duck with Cumin & Honey	15.00
Veal Tournedos with Wild Mushrooms & Brown Sauce	16.00
New York Steak with Watercress & Brown Sauce	16.50
Filet Mignon with Green Pepper Corns	16.50
Loin of Venison with Apricot Compote	18.00
Loin of Veal with Wild Mushrooms Rosemary & Cream Sauce	18.50
Lamb Noisettes with Rosemary	19.00

Poissons

Virginia River Trout Suatéed with Capers	$13.00
Filet of Rockfish with Lemon Butter	14.00
Norwegian Salmon with Watercress Cream Sauce	14.50
Sea Scallops & Roe with Old-Fashion Mustard & Cream Sauce	15.00
Half a Loster, Jumbo Shrimp & Sea Scallops Beurre Blanc	18.00
Maine Lobster Beurre Blanc	18.00

Maryland: Rockville
MISTY HARBOR
Seafood $

Hope springs eternal for a new seafood restaurant that knows and cares how to deal with fresh fish. And hope is rewarded by Misty Harbor, big and somewhat bare, with a slightly nautical air from the pictures on the wall of seagoing vessels. The setting and the service offer few frills, but the fish is very good—and that's what ultimately counts. Go for the simplest: oysters on the half-shell; broiled rockfish or flounder, stuffed with crab meat if you like; or imperial crab, large snowy lumps in just enough creamy dressing. Fried oysters, too, are plump, fresh and covered with a light and crisp batter. The same goes for the fried clams, though they are apt to be chewy. You can forgo the soups (clam chowder is thick enough to eat with a fork) and lobster dishes, since the meat is tough and tasteless. The french fries are stolid and the coleslaw heavy and oversweetened. The rule of Crisfield's applies here: concentrate on the oysters, clams, fresh fish of the day and crab imperial or stuffing—and emphasize the local. Those cautions, especially given the low-to-moderate prices for large portions of fresh seafood, will send you off pleased that you wandered off Rockville Pike for Misty Harbor.

MISTY HARBOR, 184 Rollins Avenue, Rockville, Maryland. Telephone: (301) 881-1166. Hours: 11 am–9 pm Monday–Thursday; 11 am–10 pm Friday; 4 pm–10 pm Saturday; 4 pm–9 pm Sunday. Cards: MC, V. Reservations accepted only for parties of eight or more. Free parking lot. Full bar service. Wheelchair access.

Maryland: Rockville & Bethesda
Virginia: Springfield
O'BRIEN'S PIT BARBECUE
American (Southern) $

O'Brien's has combined the most American of food, style and service in its pit barbecue restaurant. It is a cafeteria. It is a cowboy-ultramodern-plastic setting. Though its food sometimes shows the effects of expansion into new locations, it serves some of the best ribs and chili you'll find north of the Virginia Statehouse. First, O'Brien's meats taste of smoke straight through, are tender without being dry and are served in big portions. Second, the sauce, which you ladle on yourself, is a wonderful deep brown essence of tartness and savoriness that is hot but not jarring. It is good enough to sop up the dregs with your Texas toast. You can get barbecued chicken, beef, pork or ribs, but the ribs are the star. You can also get outrageously good chili, plenty hot and not too thick, with the bite left in the beans. You help yourself to fine potato salad heavy on the pickle relish, crisp coleslaw that is happily not sweetened, and beans that also deserve compliments for their lack of sugar. All of this is to be washed down with beer in a big frosty mug that is unexpectedly but appropriately a perfect plastic copy of the real thing.

O'BRIEN'S PIT BARBECUE Rockville location: 1314 East Gude Drive, Rockville, Maryland. Telephone: (301) 340-8596. Bethesda location: 7305 Waverly Street, Bethesda, Maryland. Telephone: (301) 654-9004. Hours: 11 am–10 pm Sunday–Thursday; 11 am–11 pm Friday, Saturday. Cards: MC, V. Reservations suggested for large parties. Parking lot. Full bar service. Wheelchair access.

Maryland: Potomac
OLD ANGLER'S INN
French

$$$

Dining on the terrace, with trees and a small waterfall as backdrop or sipping a drink on a sofa before the fireplace, the romance itself at Old Angler's Inn is worth the tab. Sometimes the food is, too, and at the very least it is good enough not to disrupt your reverie. If your budget allows, start with fresh foie gras, lightly sauteed with strands of ginger in a buttery sauce. More mundane choices still emerge festively garnished and quite decent: shrimp are plump and sauced with a cold lobster mousseline for a change, and soups are flavorful. Main courses, too, are prettily presented, and offer a choice of fresh fish or simple grilled meats and a couple of trendy dishes such as sliced duck breast with cassis. Probably the best choices are fish, particularly the plainest of those. The wine list is expensive but not so much as it once was. In its enchanted wooded spot, this old inn is all the better for the trip.

OLD ANGLER'S INN, 10801 Mac Arthur Boulevard, Potomac, Maryland. Telephone: (301) 365-2425. Lunch: noon–2 pm Tuesday–Friday; noon–3 pm Saturday, Sunday. Dinner: 5:30 pm–10:30 pm Tuesday–Friday; 5 pm–10:30 pm Saturday, Sunday. Closed Monday. Cards: AE, CB, DC, MC, V. Reservations suggested. Parking lot. Full bar service. Jacket required in dining room.

Maryland: Bethesda
THE PINES OF ROME
Italian

$

Heydays don't last forever, so one learns at The Pines of Rome. Bethesda's trattoria still has a home-style Italian air and one of the few authentic Italian pizzas in town. Prices remain largely at the modest level. But fatigue hits the plate too often. Rely on the fried zucchini—blistery crisp—and the red or white pizza. Veal is well cooked and well priced, and tomato-sauced dishes are zesty. Order simple foods—fried vegetables, ripe cheese and pizza—with a bottle of inexpensive wine. But enter the higher menu ranges at your own risk.

THE PINES OF ROME, 4709 Hampden Lane, Bethesda, Maryland. Telephone: (301) 657-8775. Hours: 11:30 am–11 pm Tuesday–Saturday; noon–10 pm Monday, Sunday. Cards: AE, CB, DC, MC, V. No reservations. Nearby parking lot. Beer and wine only. Wheelchair access.

Maryland: Bethesda
POSITANO
Italian $$

Bread, wine and mussels would be enough. The tables at Positano are supplied with warm bread—thick squares of oiled and garlicked focaccia and crusty, chewy Italian loaves, the likes of which Washington rarely tastes. The wine list is short but reasonably priced. And the mussels marinara appetizer is plump mussels in a thin tomato broth full of herbs and sea tang. Stuffed potato dumplings and linguine with garlic, anchovies and olives are homey and delicious, but beyond that the pastas sink into vapid cream sauces that taste like boiled milk with too much nutmeg. Veal matrimonio, a mild and delicate pate of sausage and vegetables sandwiched between a veal scallop and a chicken scallop then cooked in wine, is a light and subtle dish, the best of the main courses. Besides that, order something with tomato sauce, for if Positano is doing anything well that night, it is likely to be the tomato sauce. Reborn in a new location after being exhausted by popularity, Positano has, with the touch of some magic wand, turned from restaurant phenomenon back into a nice little neighborhood restaurant.

POSITANO, 4940 Fairmont Avenue, Bethesda, Maryland. Telephone: (301) 654-1717. Lunch: 11:30 am–2 pm daily. Dinner: 5:30 pm–10:30 pm daily. Cards: AE, MC, V. Reservations suggested. Street parking or nearby lot. Full bar service.

Maryland: Silver Spring
SAKURA PALACE
Japanese

$$

Sakura is more than twenty years old and feeling fit. Through its years it seems to grow continually more Japanese. First came its wide assortment of Japanese cooking modes—tempura, teriyaki, sukiyaki, nabemono, donburi—served western style or with diners kneeling shoeless at low tables. Several years ago a sushi bar was built, the production adding a show to those eating at the bar and adding new dimensions to the menu with a wide variety of sushi, sashimi and maki zushi (sushi rolled in seaweed). Now another touch has been added: Japanese television at the sushi bar, using imported videotapes. Waitresses wear kimonos and serve with grace, though communicating is not always easy. The menu is long and complicated, with wildly varying prices that make ordering a challenge. Order teriyaki; in that category charcoal-grilled pork is juicy and savory, and the rolled, stuffed beef negimaki is a lush combination of rare meat, scallions and seasonings. Then there is an interesting range of broth-cooked dishes such as shabu shabu and yosenabe. The success of the sukiyaki depends on whether the waitress has time to attend to it. Service at the sushi bar bogs down, too, when the restaurant is busy. Order several appetizers and expect the need to be patient.

SAKURA PALACE, 7926 Georgia Avenue, Silver Spring, Maryland. Telephone: (301) 587-7070. Lunch: 11:30 am–2:30 pm Tuesday–Friday. Dinner: 5:30 pm–10 pm Tuesday–Friday; 5 pm–10 pm Saturday, Sunday. Closed Monday. Cards: AE, MC, V. Reservations suggested. Valet parking. Full bar service. Wheelchair access. Non-smoking area.

Maryland: Wheaton
TUNG BOR ✳
Chinese (dim sum) $

A week looks pretty good when it includes dim sum lunch at Tung Bor. Weekends, justifiably, are intensely crowded, for those are the days when carts of dozens of kinds of dim sum are wheeled through the dining room for the picking and choosing. Weekdays you order from a menu. In any case, the fried won tons are as delicate as origami birds, the spring rolls combine crispness and succulence, the steamed shu mai and har gow have the thinnest of noodle wraps and subtly delicious meat and shrimp stuffings, the taro balls are lacy and crisp, and the pan-fried turnovers, with glutinous dough and wonderful chunky and fragrant bits in the filling, are sensational. Service is harried and the surroundings are low on charm, but at lunch time here very little money can bring a feast of memorable tastes. Dinner at Tung Bor? Switch around your schedule and make it lunch. It would be a pity to pass up an opportunity for the dim sum.

TUNG BOR, 11160 Veirs Mill Road (in Wheaton Plaza), Wheaton, Maryland. Telephone: (301) 933-3687. Hours: 11:30 am–9:30 pm Monday–Thursday; 11:30 am–10:30 pm Friday; 11 am–10:30 pm Saturday; 11 am–9:30 pm Sunday. Cards: MC, V. No reservations for weekend lunch, suggested for large dinner parties. Mall parking. Full bar service. Wheelchair access.

東坡酒樓
TUNG BOR RESTAURANT
933-3687

DIM SUM served: Mon-Fri 11:30 am to 3 pm, Sat & Sun 11 am to 3 pm.
Tea 50 cents per person; Chrysanthemum tea 70 cents per person.

八珍糯米鶏 ( ) 8 treasures sweet rice in lotus leaves ($2.80/1)
上湯鮮蝦水餃 ( ) Sui Gow in Soup ($2.80/5)
三絲鮮蝦春卷 ( ) Spring Rolls ($2.00/2)
蠔油鮮竹卷 ( ) Bean sheet rolls ($2.80/3)
豉椒炆牛肚 ( ) Beef tripe in black bean sauce ($2.00)
鮮蝦腸粉 ( ) Shrimp rice noodle crepe ($2.80/3)
叉燒腸粉 ( ) Roasted Pork rice noodle crepe ($2.50/3)
牛肉腸粉 ( ) Beef rice noodle crepe ($2.50/3)
蠔油釀豆腐 ( ) Stuffed bean curd ($2.00/3)
豉汁釀青椒 ( ) Stuffed pepper ($2.00/3)
鮮竹釀鴨掌 ( ) Stuffed duck feet ($2.00/2)
豉汁蒸肉排 ( ) Spareribs in black bean sauce ($2.00)
蠔珠鮮蝦丸 ( ) Steamed shrimp ball ($1.60/3)
金銀蝦多士 ( ) Shrimp toast ($1.60/3)
莎尖鮮蝦餃 ( ) Har gow (steamed shrimp dumpling) ($1.60/4)
鮮蝦魚翅餃 ( )*Shark fin dumpling ($1.60/3)
好王干蒸燒賣仔 ( ) Shiu mai (shrimp/pork dumpling) ($1.60/4)
煎鶏粒粉果 ( ) Fan-fried fun gor ($2.50/3)
焗叉燒餐飽 ( ) Baked roast pork bun ($1.60/2)
蠔皇叉燒飽 ( ) Steamed roast pork bun ($1.60/2)
香滑鶏飽仔 ( ) Steamed chicken bun ($1.60/3)
羊城膶腸卷 ( ) Steamed Chinese sausage bun ($1.60/2)
時菜牛肉球 ( ) Beef ball with vegetable ($1.60/3)
干蒸牛肉燒賣 ( ) Beef Shiu mai (steamed beef dumpling) ($1.60/4)
錦鹵炸雲吞 ( ) Fried Won Ton ($1.60/4)
安蝦咸水角 ( ) Fried shrimp/meat dumpling ($1.60/2)
什錦蜂巢芋角 ( ) Taro dumpling ($1.60/2)
臘味蘿蔔糕 ( ) Radish cake ($1.60/3)
               SWEET PASTRIES
旦黃蓮蓉飽 ( ) Steamed lotus seed paste bun ($1.60/2)
層酥鶏旦撻 ( ) Egg custard tart ($1.60/2)
杭仁馬拉糕 ( ) Chinese sponge cake ($1.60/2)
香煎馬蹄糕 ( ) Water chestnut cake ($1.60/3)
煎糯米軟餅 ( ) Soft sweet rice cake ($1.60/3)

'*' Week-end only   CARRY OUT AVAILABLE

173

Maryland: Bethesda
VAGABOND
Romanian $$

Vagabond offers some French-type dishes, but why not explore its distinctiveness as the area's only Romanian restaurant? The maitre d'hotel will gladly lead you through mysteries of icre (known elsewhere as taramasalata), mititei (spiced beef sausage), gustare (a mixed hors d'oeuvre of smoked trout vinaigrette, pickled herring and eggplant puree), mamaliga (cornmeal mush), wiener schnitzel and Romanian mixed grill. These dishes are only some of the winners, for the only truly disappointing offering I ran into was ciroba de peste, a bouillabaisse relative that proved to be nondescript seafoods in a dull, milky broth topped with a couple of slices of hot chilies.

VAGABOND, 7315 Wisconsin Avenue, Bethesda, Maryland. Telephone: (301) 654-2575. Lunch: 11:30 am–2:30 pm Monday–Friday. Dinner: 6 pm–10 pm Monday–Thursday; 6 pm–10:30 pm Friday; 6:30 pm–10:30 pm Saturday. Closed Sunday. Cards: AE, CB, DC, MC, V. Reservations suggested. Street parking or nearby lot. Full bar service.

VIRGINIA

Virginia: Fairfax & Vienna
AMERICAN CAFE
American $$

See review in Washington section page 3.

AMERICAN CAFE Fairfax location: 11836 Fair Oaks
Mall, Fairfax, Virginia. Telephone: (701) 352-0201.
Vienna location: 8601 Westwood Center Drive, Vienna,
Virginia. Telephone: (701) 790-8005. Hours: Breakfast,
Lunch, and Dinner daily. Cards: AE, CB, DC, MC, V.
Reservations suggested for large parties. Parking lot.
Full bar service. Wheelchair access. Jacket and tie
required at Vienna location.

Virginia: Alexandria
BAMIYAN
Afghan $$

See review in Washington section page 10.

BAMIYAN, 300 King Street, Alexandria, Virginia.
Telephone: (703) 548-9006. Lunch: 11:30 am–2:30 pm
Monday–Friday. Dinner: 5 pm–10:30 pm daily. Cards:
AE, MC, V. Reservations suggested. Street parking or
nearby lot. Full bar service. Wheelchair access.

Virginia: Reston
BLUE CHANNEL INN
American/Seafood $$

Your introduction to the Blue Channel Inn is likely to be the cocktail lounge, for the restaurant takes no reservations and always seems to need at least five minutes to call you to a table. The dining room is right on the water, but unfortunately only the tables on the glassed porch have an unimpeded view. In all, the room looks like a polished-up boathouse, pretty but casual, with the daily specials on blackboards and no cloths on the tables. There is some very good food lurking on the overambitious menu. Start right in with crab meat, stuffed into mushroom caps. Steamed mussels, too, are cooked just enough, plump and flavorful, as well as a bargain. The fried clams are frozen strips heavily breaded and fried into stiff tasteless sticks. If you stray so far as broiled trout, swordfish or flounder, you are likely to encounter fish with a bitter aftertaste, caked with paprika and sometimes cooked to unnecessary firmness. It all boils down to your wanting either the fine crab cakes or that excellent crab imperial. The Blue Channel Inn has brought some good eating to Reston in a pleasant casual dining room, served with the flair and enthusiasm of a chorus line. It just takes some careful picking and choosing with an unwavering eye on Chesapeake Bay tradition to assure yourself of the kitchen's best.

BLUE CHANNEL INN, 11150 South Lakes Drive, Reston, Virginia. Telephone: (703) 620-6570. Hours: 11:30 am–1 am Sunday–Thursday; 11:30 am–2 am Friday, Saturday. Brunch: 11:30 am–3 pm Sunday. Cards: AE, MC, V. No reservations. Shopping center parking lot. Full bar service. Wheelchair access.

Here's a place to discover the unexpected and to understand the mystique of Vietnamese cooking, the subtle intricacy that captures the best of its French and Chinese inheritance. Start with grilled pork or beef on skewers, or shrimp on sugarcane; either is enough to share for an appetizer. Besides being marinated in a thick sweetened Vietnamese counterpart to soy sauce, the juicy skewered meats are topped with chopped peanuts and crunchy bits of onion. The shrimp is pounded to a paste with garlic and Vietnamese fish sauce, then wrapped around sugarcane before grilling. Deep-fried rice-paper-wrapped cha gio, the most popular Vietnamese appetizer, are too bland; dipping them into peppered and sweetened fish sauce helps. Vietnamese soups show the contrast of sweet and tart with a fiery kick, soft noodles and crisp shreds of nearly raw vegetables, long-simmered broths with a last-minute addition of raw beef or fish. Whatever the main dish— beef or chicken sauteed with vegetables, shrimp or stuffed squid—the presentation is colorful, the portion large, the seasoning complex.

EAST WIND, 809 King Street, Alexandria, Virginia. Telephone: (703) 836-1515. Lunch: 11:30 am–2:30 pm Monday–Friday. Dinner: 6 pm–10 pm Sunday–Thursday; 6 pm–11 pm Friday, Saturday. Cards: AE, DC, MC, V. Reservations suggested, required on weekends. Nearby parking lot. Wheelchair access. Non-smoking area, weekend only.

Beef

BO DUN $10.95

Succulent strips of beef tenderloin marinated in our unique blend of wine, honey and spices,
rolled on fresh onions then broiled to perfection on bamboo skewers.

ORIENTAL BEEF SAUTEE - *Bo Xao Rau* $10.50

Beef sautee with baby corns, snow peas, mushrooms, and bamboo shoots.

ORANGE BEEF - *Bo Nau Cam* $10.50

Beef simmered to tender in delicate spice and fresh orange juice.

VIETNAMESE STEAK - *Bo Luc Lac* $11.95

Chunks of tender beef marinated in wine rich sauce and butter, served on fresh salad.

HANOI BEEF SAUTEE - *Bo Xao Chua* $10.50

Beef sautee with cucumber, pineapple, tomatoe and onion, Hanoi style.

Poultry

GRILLED LEMON CHICKEN - *Ga Nuong Chanh* $9.75

GINGER CHICKEN - *Ga Kho Gung* $9.75

This southern dish offers marinated chicken simmered in caramel fish sauce
to tender with ginger slices.

CHICKEN IN WINE SAUCE - *Ga Nau Ruou Chat* $9.95

Breast slices cooked in light wine sauce with straw mushrooms and celery.

CHICKEN SAUTEE SNOW PEAS - *Ga Xao Dau Hoa Lan* $9.95

Quail eggs and mushrooms.

CURRY CHICKEN - *Cari Ga* $9.50

Succulent chicken drenched in our creamy curry sauce.

Seafood

MEKONG SHRIMP - *Tom Ram Man* $13.95

Big shrimps simmered with pineapple slices in a mild fish sauce lightly spiced with pepper.

FRIED FISH SAIGON STYLE - *Ca Chien Sot Ca Chua* $13.95

Whole fish fried under a thin layer of flour, served moist and lightly crunchy in red house sauce.

STEAMED FISH SPECIAL - *Ca Hap* $13.95

Whole fish steamed to perfection then bedded in a ginger brown sauce topped with oriental vegetables.

Virginia: Alexandria
GERANIO
Italian $$

In the true spirit of Italian restaurants, Geranio is uncomplicated. It is simply adorned with whitewashed brick walls and it is straightforward in its preparation of fresh foods. Upstairs and downstairs the rooms are small, with colorful pink tablecloths. Besides the menu, specials are written on a blackboard; order from that list. Soup is high art in the kitchen. Pastas are good, but those with cream sauce could use a pinch of something zesty. Fried mozzarella here is crisp, oozing, light. Veal is excellent, sauced gently and accompanied with pleasant vegetable side dishes. Look for occasional flights of fancy like cold trout in red wine, vinegar and onions. For dessert, the kitchen usually offers a single tart of unremarkable character or berries in season. But the delicacies in this house are soups, salads, veal and the chef's daily whims.

GERANIO, 724 King Street, Alexandria, Virginia. Telephone: (703) 548-0088. Lunch: 11:30 am–2:30 pm Monday–Friday. Dinner 6 pm–10:30 pm Monday–Saturday. Closed Sunday. Cards: AE, MC, V. Reservations suggested. Street parking. Full bar service. Wheelchair access.

Virginia: Washington
INN AT LITTLE WASHINGTON ✱
American

$$$

It is easy to be the best restaurant in Washington, Virginia. But move this inn to K Street and it would be right on the top rung of restaurants in Washington D.C., as well. At least if neighbors still brought the best of their home-grown vegetables and herbs, if the trout were still just out of the local pond, if the flowers in the vases and in the salads were as dewy as ever. This restaurant is a celebration of America, at least of its corner of Virginia. The most delectable of local goods are inspirations for the likes of Silver Queen corn mousse or duck with raspberries. Start with smoked trout or crab and spinach timbale for something totally Virginian, or try tiny scallops as the most subtle of ceviches. Immediately the Inn's old friends will recognize the light, true, fresh tastes that are chef Patrick O'Connell's hallmark. He has by now developed a style that is delicate but never dull, clever but not gimmicky. His sauces are clear in both texture and flavor, and his presentations are artistic but not too precious. One could fault a few things here and there: the sweet little corn muffins neither mate well with the herb butter nor serve to mop up the sauce one doesn't want to leave, and the beautiful polished tables deserve better than paper lace mats. But that is so petty in the presence of perfect rare lamb garnished with a tiny butter-sauced timbale of spinach and impeccable little whole vegetables. This very elegant but oh-so-country inn takes seriously every detail, managing a wine list of quality and a dessert cart conspicuously elaborate. In its few years the Inn at

Little Washington has established itself as one of America's finest country dining rooms and a showcase for new American cooking.

INN AT LITTLE WASHINGTON, Washington, Virginia. Telephone: (703) 675-3800. Dinner: 6 pm–9:30 pm Wednesday–Friday; 5:30 pm–10 pm Saturday; 4 pm–9:30 pm Sunday. Closed Monday and Tuesday. Cards: MC, V. Reservations suggested. Street parking or nearby parking lot. Full bar service. Wheelchair access. Jacket and tie required.

Virginia: Arlington
THE KING AND I
Thai $

Nestled next to a video arcade in a shopping strip, this small restaurant looks slightly Disneyland inside, with brightly painted walls and a colorful pagoda constructed over the bar. Along one side are "Thai Village" alcoves with low tables that look as if you must kneel at them, but actually holes in the floor under the tables allow you to sit comfortably without tucking under your feet. Staff members treat customers like guests in their home, but the special charm of The King and I comes through on the menu. Who else offers dishes such as "crying in the rain" (elsewhere called shrimp and lemon grass soup), "prawn in the mountain" or "Venice of the east"? And what description of a marinated seafood salad is more compelling than "fresh shrimps, fresh squid, forest mushroom, onion, lettuce, and chili pepper with fresh lemon juice cooked and mixed in the nice degree appetite"? Whereas the appetizers are delicious, as they usually are at Thai restaurants, the menu has evolved so that the main dishes are every bit as delectable. Satays here are particularly good; the meat is rubbed with more spices than at most restaurants and is grilled to juiciness. Among the fried appetizers, the crab balls came out more crisp than the stuffed chicken. For a cold contrast among appetizers, the "quarter rain" seafood salad lines up pretty rows of vegetables and seafoods in a chili-spiked lemon dressing. Squid is exceptional here, whether it is in a smoky oyster sauce with broccoli or more piquant with garlic and pepper. Less exciting are roast duck and curry. This is food that is light and fresh—and hot. Thai beer in abundance is warranted.

THE KING AND I, 237 North Glebe Road, Arlington, Virginia. Telephone: (703) 524-4969. Hours: 11 am–10 pm Tuesday–Saturday; 4 pm–10 pm Sunday. Closed Monday. Cards: AE, CB, DC, MC, V. Reservations suggested. Nearby parking lot. Full bar service.

Virginia: Alexandria
LA BERGERIE
French

$$

La Bergerie has a lot going for it—its Old Town Alexandria location, its spacious and comfortable setting, its warm brick environment, but most of all, a very gracious and expert staff. It is indeed a very pleasant place to dine. And the smaller room, with its old-fashioned flowered wallpaper, is particularly winning. As for the food, it is good rather than glorious, high quality rather than exciting. The menu lists a few Basque specialties—confit de canard, parillade des pecheurs, piperade—but is otherwise a standard French array of sole nantua, sweetbreads financiere, rockfish, scallops and rack of lamb, with a particular emphasis on fish. The outstanding part of the meal is likely to be dessert, perhaps a crisp, sweet tart shell filled with kiwis and strawberries on a soft custard, or a chocolate-and-vanilla gateau St.-Honore. The food is fresh, the cooking is competent, the presentation is attractive. La Bergerie is agreeable rather than spectacular, and has the good sense to price itself accordingly.

LA BERGERIE, 218 North Lee Street, Alexandria, Virginia. Telephone: (703) 683-1007. Lunch: 11:30 am–2:30 pm Monday–Saturday. Dinner: 6 pm–10:30 pm Monday–Saturday. Closed Sunday. Cards: AE, CB, DC, MC, V. Reservations suggested. Parking lot across the street. Full bar service. Wheelchair access. Jacket required.

Les Spécialités Basco-Béarnaises

La Gabure Béarnaise 3.00

La Piperrade Basquaise 5.25

Les Moules aux Amandes 5.75

Les Civelles sautées Persillées 5.75

❧

La Parrillade des Pêcheurs 14.75
(Broiled seafood plates with thin tomato and garlic sauce)

Le Filet d' Espadon frais Basquaise 14.50
(Fresh swordfish, sautéed on a bed of tomatoes, green pepper,
white wine sauce)

Les Filets de Truite de Montagne sautés Navarraise 10.25
(Fresh mountain trout filet sautéed with ham)

Le Poulet Basquaise 10.25
(Chicken basque style)

Le Confit de Canard Béarnais 11.95
(Fresh duck confit with sauted potatoes and mushrooms)

Le Filet de Porc frais en Confit 13.25
(Fresh pork tenderloin basque style)

Le Confit de Poularde Maison 11.25
(Chicken confit)

Le Tournedos Landais 18.50
(Filet mignon with goose liver, madere sauce)

Les Escalopines de Veau Biscaenne 14.25
(Veal scalopini with bayonnaise sauce)

Virginia: Great Falls
L'AUBERGE CHEZ FRANCOIS ✳
French

$$

The impossibly busy telephone, the two-week wait for reservations, the long drive home on winding roads should be discouraging. But this endearing country restaurant satisfies despite those drawbacks and even though the food is rarely outstanding. What's the secret? A rustic French environment that feels authentic, a staff that genuinely considers its patrons' welfare, a wine list with so many interesting choices and good values that you want to sip away the week, a constantly changing menu that takes advantage of the season, and a fixed-price dinner that is very reasonably priced. The pate may fall flat, but it is garnished with several small homey salads; the sauce choron may add little character to the beef, but both will be accompanied by excellent fresh vegetables. And the saumon souffle de l'auberge, a salmon fillet topped with pike mousse, is superb, year in and year out. Chez Francois also has an unusually good selection of pastries, but include in your dessert choice the house's own ice creams. From the basket of garlic toast and rye bread to the brewed decaffeinated coffee, Chez Francois makes it clear that it cares.

L'AUBERGE CHEZ FRANCOIS, 332 Springvale Road, Great Falls, Virginia. Telephone: (703) 759-3800. Dinner: 5 pm and 9 pm seatings Tuesday–Saturday; 2:30 pm and 8 pm seatings Sunday. Closed Monday. Cards: AE, MC, V. Reservations suggested two weeks in advance. Free parking lot. Full bar service. Wheelchair access. Jacket and tie required.

Virginia: Vienna
NIZAM'S
Middle Eastern

$$

You can do a lot to ensure an enjoyable meal at this small Turkish restaurant: Reserve a table, for it is truly tiny. Order ahead if there are special Turkish dishes you like—with enough notice, the chef will make anything from swordfish kebab to stuffed vegetables. And if you like doner kebab, go on Tuesday, Friday or Sunday nights, when it is made fresh in that kitchen for those times only. Any day, though, the restaurant serves— pleasantly and efficiently—sensational yogurtlu kebab, beef slices sauced with yogurt and fresh tomato sauce, seasoned with dill, on a base of diced pita bread. The menu lists several grilled kebabs, moussaka and even "surf and turf," and the cooking is at least good, sometimes excellent. A mezze platter for two, artistically arranged, is a nice sampling; the best of it is fried eggplant with yogurt, which can be ordered also as a side dish. A simple and very good salad accompanies main courses. And by all means, save room for dessert. The baklava is the lightest, most delicate version I have found, and the rice pudding is like liquid velvet. Go ahead and order both.

NIZAM'S, 523 Maple Avenue W, Vienna, Virginia. Telephone: (703) 938-8948. Lunch: 11 am–3 pm Monday–Thursday; 11 am–2:30 pm Friday, Saturday. Dinner: 5 pm–10 pm Tuesday; 5 pm–11 pm Friday, Saturday; 4 pm–10 pm Tuesday–Thursday; 5 pm–11 pm Friday, Saturday; 4 pm–10 pm Sunday. Closed Monday. Cards: AE, CB, DC, MC, V. Reservations suggested. Parking lot. Full bar service. Wheelchair access.

Virginia: Springfield
O'BRIEN'S PIT BARBECUE
American (Southern) $

See review in Maryland section page 167.

O'BRIEN'S PIT BARBECUE, 6820 Commerce Street,
Springfield, Virginia. Telephone: (703) 569-7801. Hours:
11 am–10 pm Monday–Thursday; 11 am–11 pm Friday,
Saturday; noon–10 pm Sunday. Cards: MC, V. Reservations suggested for large parties. Parking lot. Full bar
service. Wheelchair access.

Virginia: Falls Church
PEKING GOURMET INN
Chinese $

Peking duck is the highlight, as one can guess from the
name of this small, crowded Chinese restaurant. You
can order a whole or a half with no advance notice. The
duck is rubbed with honey and hung to cook in a smoke
oven, then rolled to your table on a cart and carved to
your liking—with or without the fat removed, as you
wish. Good job. The duck hot-and-sour soup is a
successful offshoot of the process. The menu also
includes a full range of Chinese dishes, but the duck
dishes, Peking Gourmet chicken and the fried dumplings
are the ones clearly above average. Also above average
is the service—suave, helpful—which reinforces the
pleasure of a moderately priced dinner.

PEKING GOURMET INN, 6029 Leesburg Pike, Falls
Church, Virginia. Telephone: (703) 671-8088. Hours:
11 am–10:30 pm Sunday–Thursday; 11 am–midnight
Friday, Saturday. Cards: MC, V. Reservations suggested
on weekends and for parties of seven or more. Free
parking lot. Full bar service.

APPETIZERS

* CABBAGE SZECHUAN STYLE	1.30
SESAME SHRIMP	3.95
SPRING ROLL (4)	2.70
EGG ROLL (2)	1.85
BARBEQUED SPARERIBS (4)	3.95
BARBEQUED PORK	2.85
FRIED WONTON (6)	1.60
FRIED DUMPLINGS (6)	2.95

HOUSE SPECIALS

*1. PEKING GOURMET BEEF 7.95
   Beef cubes in a spicy sauce-hot and
   tasty.

*2. PEKING GOURMET CHICKEN 7.25
   Chicken cubes in a spicy sauce-hot
   and tasty.

SEAFOOD

KUNG PAO SHRIMP 9.50
   Fried shrimp in a batter with spicy ginger
   sauce.

SHRIMP IMPERIAL 9.50
   Jumbo shrimp with broccoli and snow peas in
   garlic sauce.

SHRIMP WITH LOBSTER SAUCE 8.25
   Jumbo shrimp toss-fried with peas, bamboo
   shoots, mushrooms and water chestnuts.

SWEET AND SOUR SHRIMP 50
   Shrimp deep-fried in a batter with sweet and
   sour sauce.

SHRIMP SZECHUAN STYLE 9.50
   Jumbo shrimp toss-fried in a hot pepper sauce
   with green pepper and onions.

SHRIMP PEKING STYLE 9.50
   Jumbo shrimp toss-fried in a spicy garlic
   sauce.

SHRIMP CURRY 9.50

POULTRY

CHICKEN WITH CASHEW NUTS 7.45
   Diced chicken and cashew nuts toss-fried and
   seasoned in a soy bean sauce.

KUNG PAO CHICKEN 7.45
   Diced chicken with spring onion and peanuts in
   a spicy sauce.

CHICKEN SZECHUAN STYLE 7.45
   Diced chicken with green pepper and onion in a
   spicy sauce.

CHOW SAN SHIEN 8.25
   Combination of chicken, beef, shrimp and
   vegetables.

CHICKEN CURRY 7.25

CHICKEN WITH ALMONDS 7.25
   Diced chicken toss-fried with bamboo shoots,
   mushrooms, green peas and water chestnuts,
   sprinkled with almonds.

MOO GOO GAI PAN 7.25
   Sliced tender chicken with mixed vegetables.

PEKING DUCK

Long Island duckling processed in a
truly peking manner, served
with 12 pancakes. The
duck will be carved tableside.

Whole Duck 19.00

189

Virginia: Rosslyn
SHOLL'S CAFETERIA
American   **$**

See review in Washington section page 122.

SHOLL'S CAFETERIA, 1735 North Lynn, Rosslyn, Virginia. Telephone: (202) 528-8841. Breakfast: 7 am–10:30 am Monday–Saturday. Lunch: 11 am–2:30 pm Monday–Saturday. Dinner: 4 pm–8 pm Monday–Saturday. Closed Sunday. No credit cards. No reservations. Street parking. No alcoholic beverages. Non-smoking area.

Virginia: Alexandria
TAVERNA CRETEKOU
Greek   **$$**

The whitewashed walls remain as bright, the waiters as charming and efficient, the food as zesty as ever at this long-running favorite. It is still the area's most attractive Greek restaurant, and its long menu offers plenty of choices with only a few disappointments. For appetizers, try the combinations, cold or hot, or the fried cheese. Among main dishes the simplest—roast lamb, broiled fish—have that extra flair of lemon and herbs and a great deal of care in the cooking. More intricate dishes such as lamb wrapped in phyllo, moussaka or pastitsio are less successful, sometimes heavy or dry. But stuffed grape leaves are outstandingly flavored; in fact, seasoning is a strength here. Taverna remains a fresh and authentic restaurant with largely excellent food, right down to the baklava and Greek coffee.

TAVERNA CRETEKOU, 818 King Street, Alexandria, Virginia. Telephone: (703) 548-8688. Brunch: 11 am–3 pm Sunday. Lunch: 11:30 am–2:30 pm Tuesday–Friday; noon—5 pm Saturday. Dinner: 5 pm–10:30 pm Tuesday–Friday; 5 pm–11 pm Saturday; 5 pm–9:30 pm Sunday. Closed Monday. Cards: AE, CB, DC, MC, V. Reservations suggested. Street parking. Full bar service. Wheelchair access.

Virginia: Alexandria
TERRAZZA
Italian $$

The first act is the hit at this hugely popular northern Italian restaurant, at least once you have made your way through the crowded valet parking and entrance hall overtures. Terrazza suffers from success: The wait for the valet is exceeded by the wait for a table, which is exceeded by the wait for menus, ordering and food. The pastas, however, are well worth the wait. The angel-hair noodles are exquisitely fine and appropriately sauced with a Neapolitan tomato freshness. Linguine with clams is deeply aromatic with garlic and briny with fresh clams. Agnolotti are suave spinach pillows. And even if you have never liked squid, the crunchy fresh squid salad could impress you. Then the kitchen slips into overcooked fish, mushy and bitter dry veal. When the kitchen shines, though, the food, the stylish dining room with its masses of roses and the excellent and modestly priced wine list justify all your expectations of elegance.

TERRAZZA, 710 King Street, Alexandria, Virginia. Telephone: (703) 683-6900. Lunch: 11:30 am–3:30 pm Monday–Friday. Dinner: 5:30 pm till closing daily. Cards: AE, CB, DC, MC, V. Reservations suggested. Valet parking. Full bar service. Wheelchair access. Jacket required.

Virginia: Rosslyn
TIVOLI
Continental

$$

In the dramatically mirrored third-story dining room, the tables are set in niches, corners and at angles so that diners in the 175 seats have both a sense of privacy and of being right in the middle of the party. The decorations are enormous Chinese vases and sculptures, with flower arrangements to match their scale. And at the center of this dazzling dining room is the wine cellar, with its glass walls and shelves transforming it into a major sculpture. When the waiters urge a pasta dish called saracini, order the pasta they recommend. It is homemade linguine tossed with superbly plump mussels, juicy shrimp, squid rings, sweet (though canned) little clams and a buttery, creamy sauce spiked with dill and scallions. Order it for two and share it as an appetizer or make it your lunch. Other appetizers not to be missed are notably the smoked salmon and the steamed mussels served on the half-shell in a dill butter. The soups—one day the richest and creamiest clam chowder, another

ENTREES

Paillard of Veal with Lime and Tarragon   *12.95*

Breast of Chicken with Cream and Cognac "Strassbourg", Wild Rice   *11.95*

Sauteed Calf's Liver with Shallots and Raspberry Vinegar   *11.50*

Filet Mignon Flambé au Poivre   *14.50*

Filet of Red Snapper, Bercy Sauce   *13.75*

Broiled Lamb Chops Vert Pré   *14.95*

Roast Duckling with Oranges and Grand Marnier, Wild Rice   *12.7ᵉ*

Veal Scaloppine with Mushrooms, Fines-Herbes   *13.50*

Baked Crabmeat Imperial   *14.50*

Paupiette of Lemon Sole "Florentine"   *12.25*

Chateaubriand with Bouquet of Fresh Vegetables, Bearnaise Sauce (ᴿᴼᴿ ᵀᵂᴼ) *Per Person*   *16.75*

Virginia Trout Sauteed with Toasted Pine Nuts   *10.95*

Piccata of Veal Milanaise, Fettuccine   *11.50*

Broiled New York Sirloin Steak, Marchand du Vin   *15.95*

day a full-flavored shrimp bisque sharpened with armagnac—are elegant. You can also find pate, cold seafoods, baked oysters and snails with spinach among the dinner appetizers. In all, the food is quite good; sauces are deft and subtle, the ingredients of high quality. What one expects to be the highlights, though— the elaborate pastries decorating two tiers of a rolling cart—are disappointing. Those beautiful creations taste dry here, crumbly there, lacking in the butteriness or egginess or whatever might raise them to glory. Given its quality, Tivoli is modestly priced. Given its location, it has a surprising downtown sophistication. Given its beauty, its imagination and its obvious commitment to quality in service and cuisine, it manages to be a pleasure garden worthy of the name it has adopted.

TIVOLI, 1700 North Moore Street, Rosslyn, Virginia. Telephone: (703) 524-8900. Brunch: 11 am–2:30 pm Sunday. Lunch: 11:30 am–2:30 pm Monday–Friday. Dinner: 5:30 pm–10 pm Monday–Saturday. Cards: AE, CB, DC, MC, V. Reservations suggested. Garage parking. Full bar service. Wheelchair access.

APPETIZERS

Nova Scotia Smoked Salmon. Garni 6.25

Shrimp or Lump Crabmeat Cocktail 6.95

Pâté de Campagne with Green Peppercorns 3.50

Oysters on the Half Shell with Fresh Horseradish 4.50

Steamed Mussels. Marinière 4.50

Baked Oysters in Champagne 4.95

Escargots with Spinach. "Provençale" 4.50

Melon in Season 2.95   with Prosciutto 4.95

Antipasto Tivoli 4.95

Tartar Points with American Caviar 5.25

FROM THE TUREEN

Shrimp Bisque Armagnac 2.95

Cappelletti in Brodo with Julienne Vegetables 2.95

Chilled Gazpacho 2.75

Soup du Jour 2.95

Virginia: Rosslyn
WINDOWS ✱
American

$$$

Since it's only a few floors up, its sweeping window wall catches as much highway as waterway, but this is Washington's most ambitious restaurant-with-a-view. California cuisine, they call it, and the food is as beautiful as the dining room, which is considerably so, with pale nail polish colors and lacquer-shiny walls. To share as a starter, order a pizza or calzone, haughty and elegant versions that raise peasant food to delicacy. Other fine appetizers are vegetable terrine with lobster and salmon, or foie gras in any version. Among main dishes, the rack of lamb is extraordinary, but no more so than the mesquite-grilled swordfish. All the mesquite grilling is fine, from salmon to tuna to steak, though grilling smoked salmon is going a little too far. Heartier dishes such as venison and duck are beautifully executed and garnished, though light meats such as veal and rabbit have been handled less gently than necessary, and pastas have shown a heavy hand. Accompaniments are no less ambitious than the mainstays, for there are miniature vegetables and gaufrette potatoes, homemade rolls and flavored butters. And the sauces show talent. Desserts are also glorious to see, but sometimes less thrilling to eat; stick with chocolate raspberry torte, ice creams, lemon tart or creme brulee. Still, Washington's first New American restaurant of magnificence, has started out making a big splash.

WINDOWS, 1000 Wilson Boulevard, Rosslyn, Virginia. Telephone: (703) 527-4430. Lunch: 11:30 am–2:30 pm Monday–Friday. Dinner: 5:30 pm–10 pm Monday–Thursday; 5:30 pm–11 pm Friday, Saturday; 5:30 pm–9 pm Sunday. Cards: AE, CB, DC, MC, V. Reservations suggested. Free valet parking after 6 pm. Full bar service. Wheelchair access. Non-smoking area.

INDEX

RESTAURANTS REVIEWED

ETHNIC CUISINES

AFGHAN

AMERICAN

BREAKFAST & BRUNCH

FOR BREAKFAST

NO SMOKING SECTION

LIVE MUSIC

FAMILY RESTAURANTS

IT'S O.K. TO WEAR BLUE JEANS

OPEN ON HOLIDAYS

Please keep in mind that openings and hours on Thanksgiving, Christmas Day and New Year's Day are subject to change from year to year.

OPEN NEW YEAR'S DAY

OPEN THANKSGIVING

LET THESE GUIDES LEAD YOU TO THE BEST RESTAURANTS OF OTHER AREAS

The widely acclaimed series of Best Restaurants guides is a reliable source of dining information in the most traveled areas of America. Each is written by a leading local restaurant critic and each is the same size and format with menus reproduced. Guides to the following areas are either presently available or will be published soon.

____ CHICAGO & SUBURBS By Sherman Kaplan $4.95

____ HAWAII By Dorja Leiso $4.95

____ LOS ANGELES By Colman Andrews $4.95

____ ORANGE COUNTY By Herb Baus $4.95

____ PHILADELPHIA & ENVIRONS By Elaine Tait $4.95

____ SAN DIEGO COUNTY By Jeanne Jones & Dick Duffy $4.95

____ SAN FRANCISCO BAY AREA By Jacqueline Killeen et al $4.95

____ SOUTHERN NEW ENGLAND By Patricia Brooks $4.95

_ WASHINGTON D.C. & ENVIRONS By Phyllis C. Richman $4.95

These books are available at bookstores or may be ordered from the publisher, 101 Productions, 834 Mission Street, San Francisco, CA 94103. Please add 75¢ postage and handling for each book.

Name_____

Address_____

City_____ State_____ Zip_____

Check for $_____ enclosed.